Simply Chekhov

Simply Chekhov

CAROL APOLLONIO

SIMPLY CHARLY
NEW YORK

to Jim, Steven, Betsy, Heather, and Susan,

lifelong companions.

You were always with me, though I did not always know it.

Contents

Praise for *Simply Chekhov*

"Clearly written, this introduction conveys the spirit of Chekhov's work and will inspire those unfamiliar with his stories and plays to read them. Still more, it glistens with unexpected insights that will make this book a must for serious scholars as well."

–Gary Saul Morson, Lawrence B. Dumas Professor of the Arts and Humanities and Professor of Slavic Languages and Literatures, Northwestern University

"It's not easy to write Chekhov's life and, at the same time, to give a critical appraisal of his work, all in a mere 100 pages: Carol Apollonio has achieved this feat, and has done so in a sensitive, authoritative and extraordinarily readable way."

–Donald Rayfield, Emeritus Professor of Russian in the School of Modern Languages, Queen Mary University of London

"After the titanic novelists, Chekhov can seem small, sad, and harsh, a product of Russia's twilight. Moving geographically through Chekhov's brief life, pausing for the occasional cameo discussion of an exemplary masterpiece, Apollonio persuades us of the opposite: that the stories, plays, work ethic, and worldview of Anton Chekhov are joyous performance art, wondrous and resonant with dignity. A radiantly creative life, deftly lit up from within."

–Caryl Emerson, A. Watson Armour III University Professor Emeritus of Slavic Languages and Literatures, Princeton University

"Captivating and multidimensional, Apollonio's new biography of Chekhov seamlessly weaves together his life and works, making them illuminate rather than overshadow each other in a myriad of new and unexpected ways. Without being sensationalist, this book shines with critical insights and many subtle revelations regarding Chekhov's biography and artistry. Anyone–from novice to seasoned Chekhov scholar–will learn a great deal from this highly readable, thoroughly researched, and comprehensive book."

–Radislav Lapushin, Associate Professor of Russian Literature at the University of North Carolina at Chapel Hill

"Wise, lucid, compassionate, and refreshingly to the point, this is a book after Chekhov's own heart. Carol Apollonio, one of the few people to have made a serious attempt to retrace Chekhov's steps on his epic journey from Moscow to eastern Siberia, proves to be an excellent guide both to his remarkable life and to the many facets of his literary world. It is as enjoyable to spend time with her as it is with the master himself."

–Rosamund Bartlett, author of *Chekhov: Scenes from a Life*, and translator of *About Love and Other Stories*

"Carol Apollonio's *Simply Chekhov* has perfect pitch: like Chekhov himself, her work is laconic, elegant, surprising. Making use of an original geographical framework for her book, she navigates the overlap and the spaces between the comic and the dark; the ironic and the affirmative; the creative artist and the remarkable physician-patient; the intensely private man and the political, social activist. How all this can translate into the clear, brief, yet comprehensive *Simply Chekhov* is due to Apollonio's extraordinary affinity to the author and her ability to instill Chekhov's elusive, yet powerful sensibility into readers."

–Robin Feuer Miller, Edytha Professor of Humanities and Professor of Russian and Comparative Literature, Brandeis University

"'Would knowing the whole truth about a writer change our way of reading his works?' Carol Apollonio asks in this brief but rich introduction to Chekhov. We'll never know the whole truth, but the truths unearthed and organized by Apollonio do change our way of reading Chekhov. The portraits she draws of Chekhov—each connected to a different geographical space—establish connections between the writer's life and the evolution of his craft in lucid and compelling ways. Offering along the way a range of approaches to Chekhov's best-known stories and plays, Apollonio makes you want to read (or reread) all of Chekhov through her eyes, so that *Simply Chekhov* is simply the beginning."

–Elizabeth Frances Geballe, Assistant Professor of Slavic and East European Languages and Cultures Indiana University, Bloomington

"An invaluable introduction to the author who, in his own quiet way, revolutionized modern theater and reinvented short-story form. Carol Apollonio makes exquisite sense of Chekhov's creative trajectory, first by uncovering meaningful connections between his life and his work, between his literary career and his medical one, between his plays and his stories, between one short story and another. More suggestively still, Apollonio renders Chekhov's life in time in terms of his movement through space, partly, no doubt, because his peregrinations warrant it. But this strategy also calls attention to Chekhov's understanding of the impact of physical environment on the sentient beings who find themselves in it, as well as the responsibility of those beings for their environment. Guidance like this turns newcomers into discerning readers of Chekhov. Insights like these make scholars grateful."

–Cathy L. Popkin, Jesse and George Siegel Professor in the Humanities, Department of Slavic

Other *Great Lives*

Series Editor's Foreword

S imply Charly's "Great Lives" series offers brief but authoritative introductions to the world's most influential people–scientists, artists, writers, economists, and other historical figures whose contributions have had a meaningful and enduring impact on our society.

Each book provides an illuminating look at the works, ideas, personal lives, and the legacies these individuals left behind, also shedding light on the thought processes, specific events, and experiences that led these remarkable people to their groundbreaking discoveries or other achievements. Additionally, every volume explores various challenges they had to face and overcome to make history in their respective fields, as well as the little-known character traits, quirks, strengths, and frailties, myths, and controversies that sometimes surrounded these personalities.

Our authors are prominent scholars and other top experts who have dedicated their careers to exploring each facet of their subjects' work and personal lives.

Unlike many other works that are merely descriptions of the major milestones in a person's life, the "Great Lives" series goes above and beyond the standard format and content. It brings substance, depth, and clarity to the sometimes-complex lives and works of history's most powerful and influential people.

We hope that by exploring this series, readers will not only gain new knowledge and understanding of what drove these geniuses, but also find inspiration for their own lives. Isn't this what a great book is supposed to do?

Charles Carlini, Simply Charly
New York City

Preface

Ask around, and people will tell you that Anton Chekhov (January 29, 1860–July 15, 1904) is depressing. My purpose in writing this book is to expose this as a slander, and to make the reader fall in love with his work. Chekhov himself was bewildered by this characterization of his writing. Late in life, he noted in a letter:

> Alas, it is not my fault! It comes out this way against my will, and when I write, it doesn't seem to me that what I'm writing is dark; in any case, when I'm working I'm always in a good mood. It has been observed that gloomy people, melancholics, always write cheerfully, whereas cheerful writers depress their readers. And I'm basically a cheerful person; at any rate, I lived my first thirty years, so to speak, fully satisfied with life (to Lidia Avilova, October 6, 1897).

According to the writer and memoirist Ivan Bunin, Chekhov's mother and sister claimed that they had never seen him cry, even at his brother Nikolai's funeral. Compare this with young Leo Tolstoy, whose childhood nickname was "Crybaby Lev." Fun-loving not only in childhood but throughout his life, Chekhov enjoyed playing practical jokes. On one occasion in 1901, suffering from tuberculosis that would kill him within three years, Chekhov was walking down a Yalta street with Bunin. They passed a house where women's silhouettes could be seen through an open window. Chekhov says loudly, "Have you heard? It's terrible! Bunin has been murdered! In Autka [a suburb of Yalta], he was at some Tatar woman's house!" Then he turned to Bunin and whispered, "Not a word! Tomorrow everyone in Yalta will be talking about the murder of Bunin!"

This conundrum of a self-proclaimed cheerful man who writes sad things gives us the opportunity to explore our own ways of reading. How important is it to know Chekhov as a human being when we are reading his works? No data can provide a complete picture, after all, and even if it were possible, would knowing the whole truth about a writer change our ways of reading what he wrote? First of all, what people say about themselves is always complicated—no less complicated for a writer than for anyone else. That Chekhov proclaimed himself to be an upbeat, happy person should not be taken as the whole picture. Secondly, there are as many impressions of a person as there are observers. His brother Alexander reported, counter to his sister's and mother's claims, instances in their childhood when Anton cried. Thirdly, Chekhov's own statements change—he was a normal human being who had good days and bad days, just like anyone else. Some of his letters express dark moods, or even something approaching existential despair. Alexander recorded that his brother experienced a morbid premonition of death three days before his lung hemorrhage in March of 1897. Some scholars—notably the authoritative Chekhov biographer Donald Rayfield—have postulated full-on depression. The point is: the more facts we learn about the man, the more confusing everything gets—and the more human and real he becomes.

We can never know what is going on in the depths of another's heart. Literature, too, presents mysteries; there is always something more to learn once you begin to explore. With Chekhov, what we find below the surface of his works may contradict what seemed to be obvious at first glance. He completed his last play, The Cherry Orchard, in the fall of 1903 in Yalta, far from his wife, friends, and family, physically frail, suffering a whole array of painful ailments, and only months from death. The play tells a mournful tale: the collapse of a Russian gentry family, the loss of their home, and along with it an entire way of life. The family is traumatized by the loss of their only son, who drowned years before when still a child. And yet from the beginning, before he even began to write the play, Chekhov repeatedly insisted that it was a comedy or even a vaudeville. Clearly, there is a gap between what Chekhov said he thought he was doing with his writing and what people seem to be getting out of it, or say they are. Even as it presents a challenge to readers, this gap has not hindered his reputation as one of the greatest short-story writers in the history of the world—in any language—and one of its most significant dramatists since Shakespeare. His fame has continued to grow since his death—so much so, that you have picked up this little book to learn more about the life and works of this extraordinary writer.

Another epithet often applied to Chekhov's works is "boring." Here the issue is more complicated, because he often complained of boredom, and in fact, one of his most important works is entitled "A Boring Story." His characters, too, complain of boredom. Still, that is only what is immediately visible to a surface-skimming reader. The sense of tedium in Chekhov's texts may have something to do with the way he constructed his plots. Readers—at least Western readers, who prefer action-packed plots—often feel that nothing happens. Here, too, they are wrong. Take the four mature plays, *The Seagull* (1896), *Uncle Vanya* (1898), *The Three Sisters* (1901), and *The Cherry Orchard* (1904). Unlike the works that had dominated the Russian stage previously, the action in Chekhov's drama takes place behind the scenes. Onstage the audience witnesses a sequence of banal conversations and routine actions: card playing, tea-drinking, strolling in the garden. But each of the plays is anchored in a tragic event—a death that the reader or audience does not witness directly—which takes place either before the action begins, or in "real time," offstage. The sense of aftermath, or what we might call the "beforemath," or even "sidemath," dominates every aspect of the characters' experience. Characters'—and, let's face it, people's—fates are determined by things that happen offstage, out of their control. In idle conversation, someone says, "Fine weather today!" Uncle Vanya responds, "Fine weather to hang oneself!" Something very important is missing; the spectator must puzzle it out based on the words, actions, and emotions performed onstage. This drama of "indirect action" (also called, distractingly, the "theater of mood") was Chekhov's radical and enduring contribution to world theater.

In addition to foregrounding seemingly insignificant events of everyday life, Chekhov's writing features a leveling of scale between major and minor, momentous and trivial, near and far. In an undated notebook entry, he wrote: "Looking out the window at a corpse being carried by: you've died, they're taking you to the cemetery, and here I am about to go have breakfast." Distracted by breakfast, we might miss something important. Chekhov's reluctance to distinguish great from small recalls the journal that the writer's father, Pavel Yegorovich, kept during the 1890s when the family lived on their small estate of Melikhovo outside of Moscow. Anton ("Antosha") has just come home from several months convalescing in France, but that does not affect the weather, the seasons, or the flow of life on the farm. His father wrote:

> 5 May. A clear morning +12 [degrees] ®. Wonderful weather. All the trees are dressed in greenery. Midday +24 ®, +34 ®. The sound of thunder, looks like rain. Stuffy and hot. Antosha has come back from France. Brought a lot of presents. Eve[ning] +13 ®. The oats are sprouting.

The great Russian scholar Alexander Chudakov identified this leveling—not just of events but of all elements in a text—as a key principle in Chekhov's narrative poetics. The significance of what happens is not obvious—just as in life we do not understand what we experience in the moment; explanations fall short. This does not mean, though, that life has no meaning. And despite what feels random and inexplicable, in fact, everything—in life and in a work of art—is important and needed in, as Columbia University professor and Chekhov scholar Cathy Popkin put it, Chekhov's "pragmatics of insignificance."

"The master of epistemology"

Though his characters bear their own philosophies and varieties of religious belief, Chekhov and his narrator maintain a steadfast distance before the unknown. Just weeks before his death, he wrote to his wife, the actress Olga Knipper, who had asked him about the meaning of life: "You ask: what is life? That's the same as asking: what is a carrot? A carrot is a carrot, and nothing beyond that is known." Although an avowed agnostic, he was always aware and respectful of the greater universe that no human being can understand fully. If Tolstoy's writings are focused on ethics and Dostoevsky's on ontology, Chekhov was the master of epistemology; he explored, as the Russian critic Vladimir Kataev wrote, the limits of what we can know. A correspondent wonders whether there will be a "moving of the water" (John 5) to bring healing to Russia in troubled times. Chekhov responded: "There is movement, but, like the movement of the earth around the sun, it is invisible to us." It is human to crave, and to strive, to know more than we can. In 1889, Chekhov told a literary colleague, Kazimir Barantsevich: "Man has insufficient mind and conscience to understand the present day and guess what will be tomorrow, and insufficient detachment, to judge himself and others." In his late masterpiece "In the Ravine," bereaved teenage mother Lipa, carrying the body of her murdered baby, shares her grief with an old peasant man who gives her a ride home in his cart: "Tell me, Grandfather, why should a little one be tormented before his death? When grown-ups suffer, men or women, their sins are forgiven, but why should a little one suffer, when he has no sins? Why?" And the man answers, like Chekhov: "We cannot know everything, why and how. A bird is given not four wings, but two, because it can fly with two; in the same way a man is given to know not everything, but only a half or a quarter. As much as he needs to know in order to live, that's how much he knows."

Despite the temptation, it is never safe to generalize, regardless of the gravity of the subject that Chekhov or one of his characters may be discussing. There is always a layer of irony that readers ignore to their peril. This is what makes great literature different from other forms of discourse. Even an author who starts out with the goal of communicating a clear message (usually something obvious, like the fact that adultery, poverty, and murder are bad) will soon lead into complicated and ambiguous territory, and ultimately there will be no answers. Of all the Russian classics, Chekhov is the one most associated with this stance. In the fall of 1888, he wrote his friend, the newspaper publisher Alexei Suvorin:

> You confuse two concepts: *answering a question* and *formulating a question correctly*. Only the second is mandatory for an artist. Not a single question is answered in *Anna Karenina* and *Onegin*, but they completely satisfy you, because all the questions are posed correctly. The court must pose questions correctly, but let the members of the jury decide them, each to his own taste.

Chekhov's distinctive artistic identity and stance emerge from his training as a scientist. He began publishing short stories while a medical student at Moscow University between 1879 and 1884. Upon graduation, he served as a doctor, treating patients in Moscow and its rural outskirts through the mid-1880s. He was a remarkably sensitive diagnostician, and on several occasions noted by acquaintances in memoirs, he predicted the nature and timing of a person's death, including by suicide, with frightening accuracy. From early on, he was not only a healer but also a patient, and knew illness from inside and out. His sure touch in the description of physical and emotional states, and his unique writerly combination of objectivity, psychological acuity, and empathy, draw upon these two sides of his medical experience. In an 1893 letter, he penned: "Medicine is my lawful wedded wife; literature—my mistress. Of course, both get in each other's way, but not so much as to exclude each other." Even after he became a famous writer, Chekhov continued his medical practice, often volunteering his services to treat indigent peasants. In the early 1890s, he served in public health initiatives in rural Russia, notably in efforts against famine and cholera. Over the course of his career as a doctor, he witnessed and treated the full range of disease, pain, and suffering that afflicted human beings of his time. In addition to supplying him with an endless stock of subjects, plots, and characters for his fiction, his medical practice honed the objectivity and restraint that predominates in his artistic vision.

Freedom in face of censorship

Chekhov wrote most of his stories and plays during the late 19th century, a time when Russian government censorship forbade discussion of sensitive subjects in published works, particularly those relating to politics, religion, and sex. In such an environment, a story's ostensibly calm message might mask something momentous but tabooed. Aware that what interested them most could not be expressed directly, readers developed strategies to discover subversive messages in what they read. As the American scholar Simon Karlinsky pointed out, writers faced pressure during Chekhov's time from two sides—the official censorship and the literary establishment. Critics who wrote for the prestigious journals expected a certain set of liberal or radical ideas from writers—a form of "political correctness" for the time and place. But Chekhov refused to reduce his art to any particular agenda or perspective. In a letter addressed to the poet Alexei Pleshcheev on October 4, 1888, he expressed what is considered to be his credo:

> I am afraid of people who look for a tendency between the lines and who want to pin me down as either a liberal or a conservative. I am not a liberal, nor a conservative, nor a gradualist, nor a monk, nor an indifferentist. I would like to be a free artist, and nothing more, and I regret that God has not endowed me with the strength to be one. I detest lies and violence in all their forms [...]. Pharisaism, dull-mindedness and tyranny reign not only in the homes of merchants and jail cells. I see them in science, literature, among the youth ... For that reason to an equal degree I harbor no partiality toward policemen, butchers, scholars,

writers, or youth. I believe brands and labels to be prejudices. My holy of holies is the human body, health, intelligence, talent, inspiration, love and absolute freedom, freedom from violence and lies, in whatever form the latter two might be expressed. This is the program I would adhere to if I were a major artist.

By resisting pressure from the literary establishment on the one hand, and from the institutions of officialdom on the other, to communicate obvious or tendentious messages, and by observing the world around him objectively like the scientist he was, Chekhov maintained his freedom as an artist. Timeless in their portrayal of human life, his works also offer profound insights into the burning issues of his time: the changes in Russia's economy after the emancipation of the serfs; the crumbling of Russian religious and traditional values under pressure from Western and secular ideologies; the breakdown of traditional class divisions; radical changes in gender relations and the family; and the whiff of revolution to come. Chekhov's readers can learn a great deal about art, culture, history, politics, psychology, religion, and philosophy as they were practiced in Russia at the end of the 19th century and over the sweep of human history.

Chekhov's works always mean more than they say. What we learn from reading his stories and experiencing his plays feels real, not because of any externally verifiable facts, signs, or "isms," but rather through resonances with our inner life. One of his favorite expressions was "the soul of another is darkness." The things that matter most are invisible to others. His 1898 story "About Love," cites Ephesians 5:32, calling love "a great mystery." This mystery of love is inseparable from the mysteries of the soul; Chekhov's writing reveals everything that surrounds and protects this mystery—its shells—without harming its essential core. The writer's own private life, despite the abundance of letters, memoirs, and publications documenting it, remained inaccessible to outsiders in his time, as well as in ours. In questions of religion, as in other essential matters,

Chekhov refrained from making direct assertions about faith, his own or that of others. He repeatedly claimed that he had no religion. Yet his works abound in imagery from the Judeo-Christian tradition and Biblical quotations, often hidden beneath ordinary dialogue and mundane description. Chekhov's sensibility resonates most strongly with Stoic philosophy and comes through at key moments in his stories and letters through quotes from the Hebrew Bible—most notably Ecclesiastes. But the essential core of the man—of any human being—his beliefs and his soul, remains a secret.

Chekhov's "exemplary life"

This book recounts the highlights of Chekhov's biography and tells the story of his relationships with family, friends, artists, professional associates, critics, theatergoers, and readers of his time. He lived an exemplary life as a family man, writer, doctor, and public citizen. Our chief focus, though, is on his works, which transcend the trivial details of their author's life and the transient events of their time and place. We proceed on a path that, though roughly chronological, follows a geographical principle, recognizing, as Rosamund Bartlett did in her groundbreaking 2004 biography, the importance of the locations where Chekhov lived and worked. The chapters to follow situate Chekhov in a sequence of places that correspond to stages in his path as a writer. In each chapter, we consider key works that relate to these places, either because they were written there, or because they reflect a particular theme, method, or sensibility traceable to that location. For that reason, there are occasional jumps ahead in chronology, particularly when we contrast his life in the city (Moscow and St. Petersburg) with his summers in the countryside. We begin with Chekhov's birthplace, the southern Black Sea port town of Taganrog where he lived until the age of 19. In Moscow, he attended medical school and began publishing short comic stories in lowbrow magazines and papers. Once he became an established writer, he traveled for brief periods to St. Petersburg, where he interacted with the major publishers and critics of his time. Traveling through the countryside outside of Moscow and the great steppe between the city and the Black Sea, he observed the timeless rhythms of life—human, animal, and vegetative—in nature. In 1890, he unexpectedly undertook an arduous overland trip to the prison colony on Sakhalin Island in the Far East, where he conducted demographic research. He visited Western Europe several times over the last 14 years of his life, first as a tourist and later as a tubercular patient under doctors' orders. In the 1890s, he lived in Melikhovo, a small estate he purchased outside of Moscow, where he wrote such major works as "Ward No. 6," "The Black Monk," *The Seagull,* "Peasants," and *My Life.* There he gardened, developed his property, and contributed actively to his community. Illness drove Chekhov to Yalta at the end of the decade, where he built the "white house" that would later become the Yalta Chekhov museum. There he wrote his last masterpieces, living in isolation from family and friends, far from the theatrical world that his plays would transform forever. His last journey took him away from his homeland to the German spa town of Badenweiler, where he died on July 15, 1904.

Each of these places and times is associated with a distinctive body of writing and with patterns that resonate through Chekhov's works of all periods. As we trace the key moments in his life path, we pause along the way to consider various approaches to reading these works, with the goal of moving beyond the obvious mundanities of the surface to the profound mysteries beneath. In some cases, we probe deeply into works of different periods that exemplify distinctive patterns related either to the location, or to a particular time in the writer's life. My ideal reader keeps a little pile of Chekhov stories handy and binge-reads them in between my chapters (of course all readers, from novices to fanatics, are welcome). Though Chekhov wrote some long prose works, he never produced a great hulking novel like those of his famous contemporaries and predecessors, such as Leo Tolstoy, Fyodor

Dostoevsky, or Ivan Turgenev. What to read? The easy answer is that you can't go wrong with any Chekhov story. But a more helpful answer is that if you can't read everything, then start late and long: I'll venture to say that nearly every late work is a masterpiece, and the longer the better. Starting from 1888 or so, you can't go wrong, and things get extremely profound in the mid- and late 1890s. The best editions of Chekhov's works, and online sources, provide dates for individual works, which can help orient the reader chronologically. There are hundreds of stories; a superb source is Cathy Popkin's collection, *Anton Chekhov's Selected Stories*. Longer stories not included in this edition can be found in the Pevear-Volokhonsky translation of *Seven Short Novels* and other collections; the best anthology of early comic writings is Patrick Miles and Harvey Pitcher's *Early Stories*. Also essential are one or two collections of the dramatic works containing, at a minimum, the four major plays. Online sources such as Wikipedia and Project Gutenberg can be valuable as a starting point, though not all online texts are complete, well translated, or reliable. At the end of the book, I provide a list of recommended editions, as well as biographical and critical works.

"A unique poetic and dramatic genius"

The point in all of Chekhov's writing is not plot, character, or "message," which are always just individual components contributing to the larger organic unity of his art. We do not read Chekhov to learn some particular thing; we read him because the experience of reading is so good for our soul. Each work offers a complete world in its own right, and the best way to read not only the plays, but also the short stories, is to enter this world fully. See, hear, touch, smell, and taste as the characters do. Consider the story's text as a script that only comes to life when staged—reconstituted in your mind.

It should come as no surprise that Chekhov was drawn to the drama throughout his life. As a boy he would sneak into the theater in his hometown—theater-going was frowned upon by his school's administration—and watch plays and concerts from the cheap seats at the back. His prose works often feature dramatic construction: stage directions, dialogue, and a progression from one scene to the next in chapters that correspond to acts in a play. Chekhov's career began and ended with playwriting; his earliest works were short vaudevilles and dramatic monologues written during his high school years that have been lost. His first long work that we know about is a play entitled *Fatherlessness*—later lost—that he authored at the age of 18, and his last literary work is the sublime 1904 dramatic masterpiece *The Cherry Orchard*. One-act plays and monologues written during his early years are still performed today. His four famous plays, then, can be seen as the culmination of a lifelong artistic effort—not to revolutionize the stage (as it turned out he did)—but simply to actualize his unique poetic and dramatic genius. Their extraordinary power draws upon elements of his own biography—for example, the theme of homelessness that dominates the plays, and the refrain of *The Three Sisters*, "to Moscow! To Moscow," written in Yalta and reflecting the distance that separated the playwright from his colleagues, friends, and wife. Importantly, though, these elements and repeated phrases also convey a universal human experience of isolation and longing—which is why these works live on beyond their time and place, and why you read them today.

Chekhov's stories and plays work not merely by communicating an idea or an experience, but musically, through repeated motifs and poetic language. His works offer symbols (such as the famous "seagull" and the "breaking string"), but these enigmatic images and motifs can never be indexed to one particular meaning. Chekhov told one colleague that he paid special attention to the endings of his paragraphs and chapters, making a point of selecting words by their sound, "seeking something like a musical culmination of the phrase." The great theater director Vsevolod Meyerhold understood this musicality of Chekhov's works from the very beginning, at a time when viewers and even theater professionals were baffled by his plays. After seeing a performance of The Cherry Orchard in 1904, he wrote to Chekhov: "Your play is abstract like a Tchaikovsky symphony. And a director must capture it above all through sound."

As you read the chapters to come, keep in mind that the point of learning about Chekhov is to nurture your appreciation of his art. Experience his works much as you would a musical performance. Begin with popular songs—the early two-pagers—and proceed on to recitals and chamber concerts—the short stories. Then curl up and spend an evening or two with the long mature prose works, the symphonies. Read the plays and then watch performances of them, whether on stage or in the many films that have taken Chekhov's works as their inspiration. Each performance offers new ways of understanding the text and reaches your soul in unexpected ways. These writings are his gift to us. Savor them as one great organic masterpiece, one that lives with every new reading, and renders unreal the barriers of ordinary time and space that we thought, until we listened, separated us from Chekhov.

Carol Apollonio
Durham, North Carolina

1. Taganrog

C hekhov's life path reflects the unique social dynamics and political transformations of his time. Until the mid-19th century, Russia's economy had been primarily agrarian, relying on the labor of serfs who were bound to the land. Until serfdom was abolished in 1861, there had been very little social mobility among the classes—peasants, tradesmen, merchants, clergy, and nobility. Anton Pavlovich Chekhov was born on the eve of the emancipation, on January 29, 1860, the grandson of a former serf, Yegor Mikhailovich Chekhov, who had bought his family's freedom some 20 years before and had made his way into the tradesmen class. Interestingly, Yegor's master was a Count Alexander Dmitrievich Chertkov, himself the great-uncle of a literary man, the Vladimir Chertkov who became Leo Tolstoy's disciple or evil genius (depending on whom you ask). Anton and his five siblings all rose from their lower-class roots, obtained higher education, and entered the intelligentsia (the educated professional class) as writers, artists, teachers, journalists, and civil servants—though with widely varying degrees of success. Despite considerable intellectual and artistic gifts, the two elder brothers—Alexander (1855-1913) and Nikolai (1858-89)—suffered from alcoholism and erratic work ethics, led chaotic domestic lives, and, in the latter's case, died young, at 31. Anton's life path represents the opposite extreme: an extraordinary body of work, an exemplary record of public service, and a place of honor in the Russian pantheon. Anton's younger sister Masha (1863-1957) and brother Ivan (1861-1922) became schoolteachers. The youngest sibling, Mikhail (1865-1936), had literary aspirations, whose notable fruit is his much-cited memoir of Anton.

The Chekhov siblings' life paths reflect changes taking place over the last four decades of the 19th century, a time when the inexorable forces of westernization, secularization, and modernization were clashing with traditional Russian cultural and religious values and the country's rigid, age-old autocratic system of government. These tensions simmered up in a series of protests, terrorist acts, and rebellions. In 1917, the Bolshevik Revolution brought the whole edifice down: a country was wiped off the face of the map, its leaders murdered, its religion repudiated, its economic system ruined, and its cultural traditions destroyed. In retrospect, the Revolution is an obvious historic event, but in Chekhov's time, no one could have predicted its form or magnitude. His writing, calm and uneventful on the surface, but seething with suppressed anxieties and tensions, conveys the unique spirit of the time, the pervasive unease of a doomed world.

A tormented but creative childhood

Anton Chekhov's life spanned these end times. His father, Pavel Yegorovich Chekhov (1825-1898), ran a shabby shop in the town of Taganrog, a town on the Azov Sea, off the northeastern end of the Black Sea. Taganrog had been a vibrant port in the 18th century and gained some notoriety when the emperor Alexander I died there in 1825, but its glory days were over by the time Chekhov was born, the third of six siblings (one younger sister died when a toddler). This large family subsisted in cramped, dirty, cheap quarters, and though eventually, they were able to move into their own small house, the finances were never secure and the debts piled up. Pavel Yegorovich's parenting style reflected a need to keep his struggling business afloat, a desire to set his offspring up for successful careers, no tolerance for the spontaneous joys and pastimes of childhood, a reliance on the rod, and a truly stunning degree of pedantry that manifested itself in a strict devotion to the rituals and letters of Russian Orthodoxy. He dragged the children out of bed before dawn and kept them up late at night to attend church services, and he forced the three eldest brothers, Alexander, Nikolai, and Anton, to sing in the church choir he directed. Their "angelic voices" delighted the parishioners, but masked a profound misery, and none of the boys embraced the Orthodox faith. Later, Anton wrote to a friend that when he and his brothers sang in church, "everyone watched us with tender emotion and envied my parents, but at the time we felt like little convicts."

Despite his flaws, Pavel Yegorovich managed to get his children enrolled in school in Taganrog and keep them funded there. Before and after school, the elder sons had to toil in the shop, do chores, study, and rehearse with the choir. According to their later recollections, Pavel Yegorovich reacted to his sons' slightest failure at any of these enterprises by beating them viciously. The three elder boys looked back upon their childhood in Taganrog as a relentless series of torments, including physical violence. Because of the hours they spent in rehearsals and shop duty, they had never enough time for homework, which is the likeliest explanation for an occasional failed class, even though the boys were remarkably talented: Alexander was intellectually gifted, and Nikolai was a superb natural artist and musician.

During the summer, when school was not in session, the three brothers indulged in standard provincial amusements: they fished, captured and sold songbirds, traveled through the steppe to visit relatives, performed in amateur theatricals, and indulged in the usual pranks of childhood, and later, teenage romances. Significantly, Anton was able to attend an impressive variety of productions in the Taganrog theater—concerts, operettas, operas, and plays, including performances by European luminaries on tour. In Taganrog he first saw Offenbach's opéra bouffe *La belle Hélène*, which echoed years later in *Uncle Vanya*; Shakespeare's plays, especially *Hamlet* and *King Lear*, which were to leave their mark on later classics such as *The Seagull* and "In the Ravine"; the plays of Alexander Ostrovsky; and many other productions. Anton wrote short pieces for a school journal he founded, and joined the Taganrog library, where he was able to read works by writers not on the curriculum. At the age of 19, not unpretentiously, he offered a list of recommended readings to his brother Mikhail: Harriet

Beecher Stowe gave him an over-sweet impression, as though he had eaten too many raisins, but he approved of Miguel de Cervantes' *Don Quixote* and Shakespeare, as well as works by Turgenev and Ivan Goncharov.

Chekhov's trips into the countryside around Taganrog during his teen years and subsequently, when he returned to his hometown during vacations, were formative. Visiting relatives and acquaintances in the steppe, he immersed himself in nature, as though stocking up energy for the complexities and demands of life ahead. During one of these visits at the age of 15, he fell seriously ill with peritonitis, an experience that likely influenced his later decision to study medicine. This illness left physical aftereffects that persisted throughout his life, including chronic abdominal distress, a cough, hemorrhoids, and headaches. Chekhov's early exposure to nature was formative; during his visits to and through the steppe, he gathered a great store of impressions for his future writing, most notably the 1888 masterpiece *The Steppe*. Nature description played a vital role in his mature stories, with their distinctively porous boundaries between characters' inner lives and the natural world.

The growth of the railroad network in Russia beginning in mid-century was part of a complex of macroeconomic trends that contributed to Taganrog's decline as a port town, making it challenging for shopkeepers to stay afloat. And Pavel Yegorovich's gifts, such as they were, did not run to business management. The short version of what is a painful and complicated saga is that in April 1876 he had to abandon his shop and house and flee to Moscow to avoid being thrown into debtor's prison. With him went his wife, Chekhov's mother Yevgenia Yakovlevna (1835-1919), the two elder brothers, and the two youngest children. Importantly for our story, Anton stayed behind, first with the next brother, Ivan, but then, ultimately, alone. At only 16, this schoolboy was tasked with completing his education in the Taganrog high school; fending off debtors; handling legalities related to the family home and shop; and dealing with whatever emotional challenges his circumstances inflicted upon him. Incredibly, Anton's tasks included earning money through tutoring and selling off the family's furniture, to send to his parents and siblings in Moscow. His lifelong role as chief provider for the entire family began during this trying time.

The factors creating a great artist are never completely intelligible, but there is no doubt that these three years on his own in Taganrog had an incalculable effect on Chekhov's character and set a firm foundation for his path as a writer. During this period he cultivated the remarkable set of qualities that made such an impression on his contemporaries, critics, and readers: a mighty work ethic; a sense of mature responsibility for the welfare of his parents and siblings; a remarkable independence of thought; an ability to rise above circumstance; a habit of quiet philanthropy; a sense of dignity and self-respect; a gentility of dress and demeanor—all attributes that his elder brothers, though equally talented, never possessed. Unlike the others in his family, Anton did not whine, complain, or blame fate for his lot. He held it in, did his duty, contributed what he could, argued with creditors, and did his schoolwork. Somehow, along the way, he began to write.

"The snake who swallowed the egg"

The trials of his early years left important marks on Chekhov's writing. Above all, his life in Taganrog, particularly during the crucial three years when he lived there alone, honed habits of discipline that sustained him throughout his writing career; for Chekhov, writing would be first and foremost a job, the most efficient way to earn desperately needed money to support his family. His brothers lacked that discipline, and the talents they manifested in their earlier years fell like a ray of light into a deep pit—as the self-pitying Uncle Vanya would later say about his own gifts. Secondly, the environment provided Anton with a lifetime's stock of subjects—the countryside, the schoolroom, the courthouse, the dreary town square, the farmyard—and characters: schoolteachers, police constables, peasant craftsmen, and shopkeepers—not least his own father. Compulsory daily church attendance and choir singing provided a rich matrix of verbal material (liturgy and biblical texts), which permeated his stories and intermingled there with the sounds of provincial life and of nature. Chekhov's fine ear captured the distinctive speech patterns of the local tradesmen, peasants, and provincial clergy; the noises made by domestic and wild animals and fowl; and the sounds of singing, prayer, and church bells. These sounds resonate throughout his writing, from short works like "The Requiem" (1886) to "Easter Eve" (1886) and "The Student" (1894), and culminating in the sublime music of "The Bishop" (1902). His characteristic "objective" poetics does not prioritize any one of these kinds of sounds. Human speech, bubbling water, hoofbeats, a gunshot, barking and braying, thunder, a sermon—all contribute their motifs and melody lines to the symphony of his writing.

Taganrog provided material for Chekhov's stories and offered an array of plot templates. Take "The Chameleon" (1884), whose matrix of plot, character, and setting offers a pattern that we might depict graphically as the "snake who swallowed the egg:"

A police superintendent—"Bonkers"—strides across a deserted provincial village square, followed by his deputy, who is holding a sieve full of "confiscated gooseberries." It is nap time and there's not a soul in sight. A little dog scampers onstage, limping, with a man—the goldsmith "Oinker"—in hot pursuit. The dog has bitten the man. A sundry crowd gathers, watching along with Chekhov's readers as the police superintendent attempts to discover the answer to the great Russian "accursed question": who is to blame? Various townspeople offer up speculations; the policeman adjusts his demeanor, judgment, and proposed punishment to the social class of the dog's presumed owner: lower-class—vicious brute; "the general"—cute little pup. Once it is determined that the dog belongs to a rich landowner, it is clear that no blame will be assigned. The policemen continue on their way, and the story is over. Not much happened, and nothing changed. But there is a lingering, subtle taste on the tongue, and everyone has something to think about.

The structure is simple: a static and expectant scene; two or three main characters; a gawking crowd offering colorful, running commentary; a central incident with comic and satirical tonality; and a return at the end to the static scene where the story began. This basic "snake who swallowed the egg" plot will serve Chekhov repeatedly, along with a few other simple distinctive structures, from the short early stories to the complex mature prose.

The theme of homelessness

The Chekhov family's flight to Moscow establishes a prominent theme of homelessness in the writer's major works. As his characters carry on their mundane routines, their house's foundation crumbles invisibly under them—as does that of Russia's entire landowning system. Chekhov's most poignant characters, like widowed Olga and her daughter Sasha at the end of "Peasants" (1896), wander the great Russian land from village to village like the "fowls of the air" who neither sow nor reap (Matthew 6:26). They are peasants; they begin and end with nothing. But homeless former landowners also haunt the margins of his works, such as the mocked "sponger" Ilya Telegin in Uncle Vanya, whose family, it turns out, originally owned the estate that now belongs to the play's protagonists. If homelessness is a misfortune, though, the dispossessed are never absolved of responsibility. Poor management, an ingrained sense of privilege and impracticality, and bad habits (squandering, gambling) doom the gentry—both in Chekhov's works and in his country. Underlying their collapse is the loss of the free peasant labor that up to mid-century had sustained their way of life. It remains only in scraps–the loyal old servant, Firs, forgotten and locked in the abandoned manor house at the end of *The Cherry Orchard*; the old nanny Marina in *Uncle Vanya*.

Chekhov also depicted the opposite, parallel process–upward mobility, the acquisition of mismanaged property. The lower-class, immoral, fertile, and energetic Natasha marries into the three sisters' family and, like a terrifying, organic force of nature, inexorably forces them out of the house by play's end. *The Cherry Orchard*'s Lopakhin rose from lower-class origins and through practicality, smarts, work ethic, and prudence becomes master of the estate. Lest he be judged harshly, it should be noted that he is one of Chekhov's most distinctively autobiographical characters. Indeed, unlike many other Russian writers of his time, Chekhov did not stereotype merchants or business professionals–or in fact any particular social class; his focus was on the whole human being. In "A Woman's Kingdom" (1894), a young woman of lower-class origin, Anna Akimovna, inherits a thriving factory from an uncle, gaining a level of wealth far beyond her capacity to understand. But she has no practical abilities and cannot manage money, which renders her vulnerable to the machinations of predators. On Christmas day, she impulsively gives the entire sum of cash that had been earmarked to distribute to the poor as charity, to her already wealthy lawyer, after an evening of drinking and fine dining. Chekhov refrained from editorializing in his stories about irresponsible money management; he let the facts stand for themselves. And there is enough irresponsibility to go around: dispossessed peasants squander their opportunities through drinking and debauchery; upwardly mobile characters prove unequal to the tasks of managing their new wealth; and taking advantage of the owners' lack of vigilance, unscrupulous middlemen, lawyers, and merchants, siphon off funds and property. Underlying it all is Chekhov's own bitter experience cleaning up after the mess his father made with the family's finances.

Though Chekhov left Taganrog behind, as he left behind his childhood, he did not forget or forsake his hometown. When he finally gained financial security, he "paid it back" by donating to the library, providing tuition subsidies to students, and helping the town erect a monument to its founder, Emperor Peter I. The tiny house where Chekhov was born has been preserved and is now a Chekhov museum, on what, upon the writer's death in 1904, was renamed Chekhov Street.

2. Moscow

Interestingly, even as the burdens on him in Taganrog increased, Anton's grades improved. When he graduated from high school, the city council granted him a stipend to study medicine at Moscow University. In August 1879, he left for Moscow.

The Chekhov family had been subsisting in a series of squalid rented lodgings in the city's less desirable neighborhoods. With Anton's arrival, they took in lodgers and their dire state of poverty began to ease—though the area where they lived, Grachovka, was notorious for its crime, drinking dens, and brothels—the latter to be the subject of his famous 1889 story "An Attack of Nerves" (or "Seizure" or "Breakdown"). Nikolai had enrolled in the Moscow School of Painting, Sculpture, and Architecture, and Alexander was completing his studies in natural science and mathematics at the university. Anton passed his entrance exams to medical school and began attending lectures in the fall.

Alexander and Nikolai had established connections with various weekly magazines—not the "thick journals" where Russia's major writers published their great novels, but what was known as the boulevard press, lowbrow periodicals providing light entertainment for the newly literate lower middle classes. Their genre was a weird Russian combination of *Mad Magazine*, *National Lampoon*, zines, and supermarket tabloids. Aspiring writers who were able to create articles and stories fitting the necessary formulae could earn pocket change—but not much more. Through a combination of persistence, talent, and personal connections, Alexander and Nikolai had had some success placing short prose pieces, anecdotes, and illustrations in such outlets as *The Dragonfly*, *The Spectator*, and *The Alarm Clock*. Back in Taganrog, Anton had been a regular reader of these periodicals, and had begun sending manuscripts there, which were roundly rejected. Finally, though, after he relocated to the city, editors began to accept his contributions. In March 1880, he succeeded in placing two pieces in *The Alarm Clock*: "A Letter from a Don Landowner to a Learned Neighbor"–an imitation of a provincial pedant's pompous epistolary style, which not coincidentally resembled his own father's. The second story, "What we Find Most Often in Novels, Stories, etc.," offered, as the title implies, a listing of literary clichés–characters such as a countess (a faded beauty), an impoverished landowner, dull-witted lackeys; settings including a mortgaged estate, a dacha outside Moscow; props like a Russian-leather briefcase, Chinese porcelain, champagne, a revolver that never misfires; plots featuring eavesdropping, no ending, a wedding at the end. The whole piece totals 214 words–mere kopecks for its budding author. Interestingly, though young Chekhov's aim for the piece was comic and irreverent, most of the elements he listed can be found in his future works–albeit with a radically different tonality.

The demands for fresh material were relentless. Chekhov found his stories and characters everywhere, including close to home. In "The Wedding Season," published in *The Spectator* in 1881, with illustrations by Nikolai, the two brothers lampooned–and deeply offended–their Taganrog relatives, who in good faith had invited and hosted them at a family wedding. This was the first but not the last time Chekhov hurt people close to him by utilizing details from their lives in his writing. His channeling of episodes from his friends' personal lives into "The Grasshopper" (1892) and *The Seagull* are notorious examples. The detachment that most of the people close to Chekhov observed in him allowed him to use them as fodder for his art, and betray not the slightest contrition for doing so.

By 1882, he was writing regularly for the boulevard press. Whatever his literary ambitions, he wrote primarily for money, during the time available from his medical studies. He signed his work with pseudonyms, saving his name for serious academic research that he hoped to write someday. During this period, Chekhov honed a set of skills that would serve him well throughout his writing career–he had to produce quickly, to strict generic specifications and word limits, under deadline. The need to entertain his lowbrow reader meant that the dominant tone of his early works was comic, often with an admixture of benign satire. He published some longer stories during this period, but most of his works were necessarily very short. He generally did not have the time or space to develop a single theme, an extended plot, or set of characters. At one point during this early period, Chekhov wrote to one of his editors, Nikolai Leikin: "All human life consists of trivial details." `He channeled this trivia of life into his early stories, which were often not much more than anecdotes, jokes depending on a clever punchline or amusing premise. Many of them were masterpieces of the genre. One famous example is the 1883 story, "The Death of a Government Clerk." A low-ranking clerk with the comic name "Wormy" is attending a theatrical performance when he accidentally sneezes, spattering the bald head of a "general" in the civil service seated directly in front of him. Terrified of the potential consequences, he goes repeatedly to the general's office to apologize, provoking the man into a rage, whereupon he skulks home and abruptly "...kicks the bucket."

Eventually, Chekhov had enough material to put together his first book in 1884, a collection of stories relating to the theater, which he entitled *Tales of Melpomene*. Other volumes followed—*Motley Stories* (1886) and *In the Twilight* (1887), but as was the standard practice for 19th-century Russian writers, Chekhov continued to publish individual works in the periodical press. As he developed a name for himself, he moved into established newspapers such as the St. Petersburg-based *New Time* and *Petersburg Newspaper*. Later, he was to progress to the highbrow thick journals that focused on serious literature. In the early and mid-1880s, though, the boulevard press was his main outlet. He signed his short pieces with a variety of pseudonyms: Antosha Chekhonte; The Man Without a Spleen; Doctor without Patients; My Brother's Brother; various configurations of initials; and many more. Explaining his use of pseudonyms to a literary colleague, Viktor Bilibin, on February 14, 1886, he wrote, "I have given my real name to medicine, from which I will not part to the very grave. Sooner or later literature and I will have to part ways. Secondly, medicine, which imagines itself to be serious, and the game of literature must have different nicknames."

The incredible efficiency of language Chekhov developed during this time was not merely a product of writing within short time constraints and deadlines; it quite directly reflects the brutal fact that he was paid by the line under strict length limits and had to squeeze maximum impact from each word. The early 1880s, when he was writing intensively during intervals between his medical studies, served as a literary apprenticeship that would give him everything he needed when he was finally able to write for a sophisticated reader. He could write anywhere, any time. The writer Vladimir Korolenko reported a conversation with Chekhov about his creative process: "'Do you know how I write my short stories?' He looked around the table, picked up the first thing that caught his eyes—an ashtray—, placed it in front of me, and said: 'If you want, tomorrow there will be a story ... entitled "The Ashtray."'" Chekhov claimed that he wrote one of his most famous early works, "The Huntsman," in a bathing shed. The circumstances in which he wrote would be unimaginable for established writers of the nobility. In 1883 he complained to Leikin:

> I write in the most wretched conditions. My non-literary work is in front of me, beating mercilessly against my conscience; in the next room the offspring of a visiting relative is screaming; in another room my father is reading aloud to my mother from [Leskov's] "The Sealed Angel." Someone has cranked up the music box, and I'm hearing "La Belle Helene." For a man of letters it is hard to think up something more wretched than these conditions.

Between August 1879, when he enrolled in Moscow University, and 1884, when he graduated and was certified for general practice, Chekhov spent most of his time attending lectures and studying. In 1884, during an arduous stint as a journalist covering a trial in Moscow, he suffered a lung hemorrhage, a precursor or symptom of tuberculosis. These episodes would plague him throughout his life, but for many years he denied their severity, until he suffered a hemorrhage in 1897 that endangered his life, finally making him admit the nature of his disease. Doctors appear often in his works, beginning in *Belated Blossoms*, an atypically long melodramatic prose work from 1882. Chekhov's hero bears autobiographical traits reflecting both the author's (projected) path of upward mobility and his medical practice. The daughter in an impoverished gentry family, ill with consumption, pines away in longing for her doctor, a man who has risen, through hard work, from lower-class origins. He realizes his love for her too late to save her life.

"A remarkable quality of balance and efficiency"

Other important influences on Chekhov during the early and mid-1880s include, in the public realm, the political climate of the period, and, in the private realm, his very active social life. The famously liberal "Tsar-liberator" Alexander II, who had presided over the emancipation of the serfs in 1861 and the subsequent liberal reforms in Russian legal and social policy, was assassinated on March 13, 1881, in St. Petersburg. The 1880s were a time of intense vigilance on the part of the authorities, particularly directed at students (who were assumed, mostly correctly, to have liberal or radical tendencies) and members of the intelligentsia, including writers. As both a writer and a student, Chekhov would arouse suspicions. Indeed, as the biographer Donald Rayfield reported, he was a target for police surveillance during this time and later, in 1887 when he traveled to his hometown, and like those of all other writers, his works were subject to strict censorship. Although he emphatically proclaimed that he was a free artist, not an advocate for any particular political program, his writings reflect ongoing tensions during this period. In stories like "Sgt. Prishibeev," "The Death of a Government Clerk," and "Fat and Thin," he treated potentially sensitive topics like police abuse of power and the dehumanizing effect of the hierarchies of rank in officialdom, without transgressing the boundaries of the permissible. The stance of objectivity and restraint that characterizes his artistic sensibility, then, drew not only upon his medical training but also the political realities of his time and place. Chekhov addressed the full range of Russian accursed questions, but in his works, they are not foregrounded as in, say, Dostoevsky's novels, where characters argue endlessly about ethics and theology, or in Tolstoy's works, where moral issues infuse every detail of plot and character. The critic Pyotr Bitsilli used the term "laconism" to characterize the artistic wholeness of Chekhov's art, a remarkable quality of balance and efficiency in which nothing is superfluous. No one issue can dominate the text. In the 1892 story, "Ward no. 6," where Chekhov explored the ethical implications of stoic philosophy, the protagonist, Dr. Ragin, spends his afternoons and evenings reading–not treating patients. In a Dostoevsky novel, when a character picks up a book, the reader will know what he is reading and why; when Chekhov's Dr. Ragin picks up a book, he also picks up a pickle and a glass of vodka–and we never know what is in the book, beyond that it is probably about philosophy or history, or possibly a medical journal:

> He reads a lot, and always with great pleasure. Half of his salary goes to buying books, and three of the six rooms in his apartment are piled up with books and old journals. He likes writings about history and philosophy the best; the only thing he reads in medicine is the journal *The Doctor*, which he always starts reading from the end. He reads for several hours on end without tiring of it. He reads not as quickly and impulsively as Ivan Dmitrych used to, but slowly, with deep concentration, often stopping at places that he likes or does not understand. Next to his book always stands a decanter of vodka, and there is always a pickled cucumber or apple lying right there on the tablecloth, not on a plate. Every half hour, without looking up from his book he pours himself a glassful

of vodka and drinks it, then, without looking, he feels for the pickle and takes a bite.

Chekhov's sense of measure, his refusal to prioritize intellectualizing over other aspects of life, would draw criticism from liberal readers who expected literature to promote political agendas. This does not mean that he did not feel strongly about various issues; his concerns for education, science, medicine, and the environment, and his ethos of individual responsibility and respect for others pervade his writing–not in the form of explicit statements, but through the examples he provided and the stories he told. How much of this sense of measure, which was one of the most distinctive characteristics of his art, was intrinsically part of Chekhov's character and scientific training, and how much of it was honed in the political circumstances of his time, cannot be calculated.

Empathy and understanding of the female psychology

Anton's social life also strongly influenced his art. The Moscow years provided him with a wide circle of acquaintances. Through his gregarious brothers and sister, he met people from various milieus, in addition to his fellow medical students: Alexander's friends from the university and in the publishing world; young artists in Nikolai's circle; Masha's friends; and military officers and landowners who lived near his brother Ivan, who became a schoolteacher in the nearby town of Voskresensk. All of these new acquaintances broadened Anton's social sphere and provided him with an endless stream of themes, characters, and plots. Some of them remained friends and, in the case of his medical school cohort, colleagues, for life and left important reminiscences. Additionally, in Moscow

Chekhov socialized with members of the theater world and felt completely at home in the city's bohemian circles.

Handsome, urbane, and with exquisite manners, Chekhov was irresistible to women, but even in serious relationships, he maintained his distance. Reflecting his training as a doctor and scientist, his depictions of women, and relationships with them, were devoid of romantic illusions. He conducted long-term affairs in the 1880s with educated women like the editorial assistant Natalya Golden–who later married his elder brother Alexander–and fellow students of his sister Masha: the "astronomer" intellectual Olga Kundasova and Dunya Efros, whom for a time he identified as his fiancée until her Jewish religion got in the way. Other liaisons were more fleeting, including in the theatrical demi-monde and in brothels, where, like many men of his generation, he was an unabashed client. Prostitution was legal at the time, and prostitutes were subjected to regular medical examinations as a public health measure, including by young doctors in training like Chekhov.

If in letters of this period Chekhov often referred to females in crude terms, his fictional and dramatic depictions manifest a deep respect for women (despite some critics' characterization of him as misogynistic) and nuanced insight into the complexity of their inner lives. His range in fictional treatments of the female experience was extraordinarily broad; with time he moved beyond the situational comedies favored in the boulevard press (betrayed husbands, shrewish wives, failed trysts and the like), into probing works conveying empathy and understanding of the female psychology, particularly when the character was helpless or abused. Several stories from 1886 offer a range of women's experience, from victim to vixen. In "Anyuta," a girl serves as a model for an art student and an anatomy study aid for a medical student, descending inexorably down the social ladder as she is passed from one man to the next. In "The Chorus Girl," a man's liaison with the titular mistress is interrupted by his enraged wife, who demands back the jewelry her husband had given his lover. Rashly, the chorus girl ends up giving the wife all her jewelry, not just what she had received from the husband. In a few cases, such as "The Witch" and "Mire," Chekhov's treatment of female sexual desire was frank and even alarming to a placid reader. The latter work roused a particularly hostile response among readers for its attribution of predatory female sexuality to a stereotypical Jewish heroine—though throughout his life Chekhov was a vocal opponent of anti-Semitism, for a time had a Jewish fiancée, and in the late 1890s broke with Alexei Suvorin, who had been one of his closest friends and associates, over the virulent anti-Semitism Suvorin expressed in his writings over the arrest and court-martial of French Jewish officer Alfred Dreyfus.

The schematic patterns that Chekhov used in his early writing in conformity to the demands of the comic journals took on depth and scope as he matured as a writer. Betrayed husbands, failed marriage proposals, edgy but hilarious encounters with police constables, sudden death—all of these elements easily flip into tragedy while retaining fundamental details of plot, character, and setting. Chekhov's distinctive "tragicomedy," or "laughter through tears," drew on the time-honored Gogolian sensibility in Russian literature, with the addition of the scientist's acute eye, objectivity, and sense of measure. His treatment of women is no exception. A frequent plot pattern is that of the "interrupted marriage proposal": A young man and a marriageable girl are made for each other. Chekhov's narrator brings them together into a romantic setting: a garden in springtime, fragrant with the scent of lilac. At the key moment, the man does not propose. In later works, there is no explanation for the man's failure; everything is perfect, but it does not come to pass. This vacuum of event, shall we call it, "non-climax," works precisely because Chekhov had so carefully arranged all the story's elements—characterization, plot tension, scenery—to lead up to the moment. Instead of resolution or closure, we feel a great emptiness, fraught with tension: what might have happened but did not. It is ever so much more powerful than the event itself would have been. The unrealized marriage proposal, which in the early stories is a funny anecdote, in the mature works takes on elements of tragedy: a vacuum opens out at the key moment, and a young woman suddenly faces a dark future of spinsterhood, poverty, and homelessness. This grim future will not be depicted; the most important thing is not said. Elements of this pattern recur in works like "Verochka" (1887), "Ionych" (1898), and The Cherry Orchard.

A responsible and orderly life

Over the five arduous years of his medical studies, Chekhov continued to support his family while learning the vast amount of material required of a doctor in Russia during that period—in its medical curriculum, Moscow University was fully up to western European standards. It is likely that Chekhov's firmly held insistence on an ethos of personal responsibility came not merely as a result of his years handling the family's business affairs in Taganrog, but also as a reaction to his brothers' disorderly, and in both cases, literally filthy, lifestyle. This sense of responsibility pervades his works, whatever their themes—homelessness, nature, miscommunication, or medicine. Dr. Ragin, the pickle-eating protagonist of "Ward no. 6," adheres to a philosophy of stoicism. The underside of this way of thinking is a lethal passivity and neglect of his duties as a physician which brings real suffering upon the patients in his care and leads to his own downfall. Chekhov had no mercy for the irresponsible and the slovenly. In key letters to his brothers, he emphasized the importance of personal accountability, culture, decorum, and cleanliness, which for him were values on the same scale. In a letter to Nikolai written in March 1886, Anton delivered an extended, eight-point lecture on how "well-bred" people ought to conduct themselves:

[...]

(3) They respect other people's property, and so pay their debts.

(4) They are sincere and fear lies like fire. They do not lie, even about small things. Lies are insulting for the listener and lower his respect for the liar. They do not put on airs, or behave on the streets as they do at home, they do not show off in front of their juniors ... they are not talkative and do not overshare on matters they are not asked about ... Out of respect for others' ears, they mostly remain silent.

[...]

(8) They cultivate in themselves an aesthetic sense. They cannot allow themselves to fall asleep fully clothed, see a crack in the wall full of bedbugs, breathe foul air, walk on a floor covered with spit, or eat off a kerosene stove. They try as much as possible to tame and ennoble the sexual instinct...

Chekhov was not judging his brother on the grounds of immorality, by the way—he himself indulged fully in the Bohemian life; rather, his emphasis was on dignity and culture. Alexander's slovenly behavior and disorderly domestic life with his second wife, Natalia Golden, prompted Anton to set forth his principles for how women should be treated. He wrote his brother in January 1889:

No matter how insignificant and sinful a woman might be, no matter how close she is to you, you do not have the right to sit in her presence with no trousers on, to be drunk in her presence, to utter words that even factory workers won't allow themselves to say when they see a woman nearby. You consider decency and decorum to be prejudices, but there must be something worth sparing, at least feminine weakness and children—to spare the poetry of life at least, if it's too late for prose.

In this long and fervent letter, Chekhov invoked their father's treatment of their mother: "I beg you to recall that despotism and lies destroyed your mother's youth. Despotism and lies crippled our childhood to such a degree that it is nauseating and horrible to recall."

In addressing facts of Chekhov's (or any person's) biography, particularly in sensitive matters like his relationships with women, family, and intimate friends, the gaps may hold more information than the available facts. The temptation to generalize from a writer's fiction, no matter how autobiographical, should also be resisted. Letters and memoirs chronicle those aspects of a relationship that are necessarily written when the parties are separated in time and space. The personal life and what happens between individuals in private remains secret. There is some irony in the fact that Chekhov treated letters he received with great care, filing them away annually into folders. Others were more careless. Before a man becomes famous, his correspondents may casually toss away his letters; this is particularly true when they do not have a permanent address, as was the case during the Chekhov family's early years in Moscow. The loss is profound. What was life like for teenage Anton, alone in Taganrog? And what about his private relationships with women? What was said in letters that were destroyed by their recipients, or by later editors, for "compromising" content? Until Donald Rayfield gained access to previously unavailable archival materials in the 1990s, including letters written to Chekhov throughout his lifetime, readers had constructed an image of the man based on the distinctively passive male protagonist of his most famous stories and plays—a quiet ascetic who either showed no particular interest in women or, like other Russian literary "superfluous men," inevitably failed at love. Rayfield's biography proves this image to be false. Throughout his life, beginning with his loss of virginity—as he claimed in a letter, at the age of 13—and up to his marriage at 41 to the actress Olga Knipper, Chekhov conducted a very active love life, ranging from casual liaisons to full-on affairs with a number of women, some of them lasting years, and some conducted simultaneously. And the language he used in his conversations and letters could be salacious, profane, and earthy. None of this is obvious to the reader of his works, and even the scholar will miss much of the picture, given the testimony that has been irrevocably lost.

A listener by nature, Chekhov was never in the habit of delivering tirades. Most of the views on life, politics, religion, Russia's fate, human nature, and art that we attribute to him come in letters. What did he say when he talked with his friends, leaving no written record? Beginning in 1888, whenever he stayed with Suvorin, the two of them talked "philosophy" for hours on end. "I haven't written a single line," he wrote to his family from Suvorin's dacha in Crimea: "All day long I eat, drink, and talk, talk endlessly. I've turned into a conversation machine." Their conversation continued in a correspondence that lasted for years and covered a range of momentous subjects—politics, views on literature, human relationships, culture, and more. But all of Suvorin's letters to Chekhov are lost—so all we have is half the conversation. Another vitally important relationship in Chekhov's life was his long-term friendship with the famous landscape artist Isaac Levitan; the two of them shared not only overlapping romantic interests, but also an important artistic symbiosis. Levitan's landscape paintings had a profound influence on Chekhov's treatment of the natural world, and their conversations and shared experiences found their reflections in Chekhov's writing. How extensive was this influence, though, we will never know: upon Levitan's death in 1900, his brother Adolf burned all his correspondence, including all of Chekhov's letters to the artist, in response to Levitan's dying wish. There are 55 extant letters from Levitan to Chekhov, but the other—Chekhov's half of their correspondence—went up in smoke.

When attempting to characterize Chekhov's lifestyle, personality, and views, then, humility is in order. There is much more that we do not know than what we do. In 1886, one Chekhov friend, Alexei Kiselyov, wrote: "The difference between my letters and yours, dear Anton, is that you can boldly read mine to young ladies, whereas I must throw yours into the stove as soon as I've read the in case my wife catches sight of them." What did Chekhov say in these letters, and in fact in all the other letters and conversations that we have no access to? What would we do with that information if we did have it? So again, we return—with some relief—to the one complete thing we do, and should, have: the stories and plays written for us.

Over the course of nine years after their arrival in Moscow in 1877, the Chekhov family had lived in a succession of up to 12 different rented lodgings. By 1886, Anton had become established as a writer and doctor, had a reliable income, and was able to settle his family into more permanent quarters. He rented a small house on Sadovo-Kudrinskaya Street, on the ring road encircling central Moscow. The family dubbed the house for its quaint appearance and red paint the "red cupboard." During the four years Chekhov lived there, he continued his intermittent medical practice and wrote for periodical publications and newspapers. From this point on, he turned away from anecdotal short pieces to the more substantial writing that would establish his lasting fame. The house became a permanent museum in 1954, on the 50th anniversary of the writer's death. The Moscow Chekhov House Museum offers an inimitable picture of the writer's daily life in the late 1880s and should be on the itinerary of every visitor to the city.

3. Summers in Nature

After Chekhov graduated and was certified to practice medicine in June 1884, he spent some weeks in the countryside assisting the doctor at a hospital near the New Jerusalem monastery in Voskresensk, where his younger brother Ivan was working as a schoolteacher. Anton's rural medical practice among local peasants provided endless subjects for stories: infectious diseases, childbirth, trauma, dysentery, and relatively minor but unpleasant procedures like pulling teeth. Among Chekhov's many works featuring the latter are two comic stories, "Surgery" (1884) and "A Horsey Name" (1885). The former describes a gruesome tooth extraction by a medical assistant substituting for his absent supervisor. In the latter, a high-ranking official suffers a terrible toothache. His steward recommends a sorcerer he knows who can cure a toothache by casting a spell, but the steward cannot recall his name beyond that it's somehow related to horses. A hilarious exchange ensues, with all the members of the household helpfully offering different horse-related names. By the time the steward finally hits upon the correct name, the sufferer has given up and had the tooth pulled. As with most great literature, the story's significance lies not in any message, but in the joy it provides readers along the way. Autopsies were among Chekhov's duties in Voskresensk; this experience is reflected in the famous 1899 story, "On Official Business," which centers on the autopsy of a man who had committed suicide. "Grief" (1886) draws on Chekhov's experience of doctoring in the countryside: an old woodworker takes his sick wife to the hospital during a snowstorm, delivering, along the way, what is partially a script for his upcoming conversation with the doctor, partially a confession and apology for his violence and drunkenness throughout their marriage, and partially a prayer or plea for his wife's health. When he turns to look at her, she is dead—her face grave and solemn (like the reader deduces, the face of a saint on a wooden Russian icon); her hand, too, wooden—like the widower's raw material.

The following summer, Chekhov rented a summer cottage (a *dacha*) from a family of impoverished nobility, Alexei and Maria Kiselyov, who were to become long-term friends. Near their estate of Babkino, Chekhov practiced medicine, took in new impressions, and wrote short masterpieces. The Kiselyovs, despite having fallen on hard times economically, appreciated the finer things in life: literature, art, and culture. Chekhov's acquaintance with them provided him with a glimpse into the lives of gentry landowners, which in due time he would incorporate into his fiction and drama. For the next few years, the Chekhovs were to spend their summers in the countryside, first in Babkino, and later in Sumy, Ukraine, where they would rent a dacha from another gentry family, the Lintvaryovs. Many of their city friends including, as time went on, eminent literati, came to visit.

The rhythm of Chekhov's travels to and through the countryside in the summer reflected a typical Russian pattern of life in accordance with the cycle of the seasons: long hard winters in the city and short, restful summers in the lap of nature. In the city, he wrote, corresponded with editors, attended the theater, indulged in the city's nightlife, and practiced medicine. Gradually he gained a readership and became able to pick his outlets for publication. After the spring thaws, he moved with various family members to the countryside for the summer. There they spent time in conversation with their hosts and friends, listened to music, and spent hours outside, fishing, gathering mushrooms, resting, and appreciating nature. During the summers he spent in the country, despite his frequent assertions that he was lazy, bored, and got no work done, Chekhov produced an extraordinary body of writing, each work more profound than the one before.

As in summers during his teen years before he moved to Moscow, Chekhov took long journeys through the steppe between Moscow and the Black Sea at various times during his life, notably in the spring of 1887—a trip that gave material for stories like "Fortune" and "Tumbleweed," which were published that year. In all these travels, he immersed himself in nature, observing the sounds, sights, and tastes of the lives of plants, animals, and human beings who lived in the countryside and the steppe. In Babkino and Sumy, he hosted many visitors: other writers and editors, family friends, and, notably, visual artists like the landscape painter Isaac Levitan and Franz Schekhtel, former fellow students of his brother Nikolai from the Moscow School of Painting, Sculpture, and Architecture. All of these relationships and impressions in the lap of nature were to have a profound influence on his art. In his play, *The Wood Demon* and its later adaptation into *Uncle Vanya*, as well as in stories like "Panpipes" (1887), among Chekhov's most appealing protagonists are environmental activists, before there was such a thing. But his treatment of the natural world moves beyond any thematic or programmatic content; Chekhov's works introduce something entirely new to world literature: a depiction of sentient beings (humans and animals) whose inner spiritual, emotional, and psychological life merges with that of the environment. His poetics moves beyond the "pathetic fallacy" practiced by the Romantics, in whose works natural phenomena reflect inner psychological states. In works of this earlier tradition, thunder and lightning, for example, might signal a character's rage or distress—but the individual's experience is always the center of attention. In Chekhov's works all human, animal, and plant life is an integral part of nature—not dominant, not separate from the natural world, but reflecting, submitting to, and interacting with its rhythms. This distinctive Chekhovian treatment of nature derives from his experiences living and traveling through the countryside; it also reflects his relationship with landscape artists during this time, particularly Levitan.

At one with nature

In this chapter, we move beyond what has been to this point a mostly chronological approach–tracking Chekhov's life path from youth to maturity–to consider Chekhov's writing in the context of his depiction of nature. He generally lived in the countryside during the summers, and beginning in the mid-1880s, his works set in nature reflect a particular and distinctive approach, whatever their time of writing. Chekhov devoted much of his free time in the countryside fishing. This particular passion left its mark on many stories, such as the hilarious early classics "Daughter of Albion" (1883), "The Burbot" (1885), and "The Malefactor" (1887), and later works like *The Seagull*. In addition to providing endless themes for Chekhov's works, fishing also served as a metaphor for his creative process. In many letters, he wrote about his "laziness" or "idleness," claiming that he was wasting his time and could not get anything done. Given his remarkable productivity over the 44 years of his life, this reads more like a fantasy than a statement of fact. But idleness, however he might have defined it, is an essential part of the creative process. The artist must clear his mind of superficial, venal, or mundane concerns and allow it, like soil, to lie fallow and absorb impressions. The other side of the creative process is hard work. Chekhov was never free of economic need; his writing was inextricably bound with the need to earn money. He committed in advance to produce work for journals, which meant he was always facing deadlines. In the early years, he committed to writing stories of a specified (short) length on certain days of the week, for various publications. Later, the pressures were different. Once he became famous, he was given the opportunity to write longer works for prestigious journals, for much better pay. This meant that he could spend more time on his craft. But the pressure remained–now compounded with the higher expectations of discriminating editors, critics, and readers, not to mention the envy of less gifted writers. And when he took on a large loan in 1892 to buy an estate in

Melikhovo outside Moscow, that expense added a new source of stress. So his complaints of "idleness" related to an ongoing sense that, no matter how productive he was, there was always more to do. But the fact is, he did take time to recharge, to rest, and to relax with friends. Fishing was the quintessential "idle" activity. The artist sat quietly on the bank for hours, gazed over the surface of the water, waited, and thought. The point was not necessarily to get a fish (Chekhov generally threw them back); the point was the listening and looking. First, he observed. Then he retreated to his desk and wrote everything down.

Chekhov caught his ideas not only while sitting quietly and listening. They came to him at all times, whether he was in conversation with friends or going about his daily routine. He'd observe a situation, or hear a phrase; or a pithy thought or scrap of language would come to him. Memoirists record shreds of conversation in which Chekhov shared these observations. One acquaintance, Nikolai Teleshov, recalled a late-night barroom conversation in 1888 with Chekhov, his brother Mikhail, and another friend. Anton said that a curious person could find a story idea anywhere,

> [...] in lemon slices that smell like onions; in greasy spots on a wall where cabbies have rested their heads: "how can it be that there are no ideas for stories?" Anton Pavlovich insisted. "Everything is a story idea, they are everywhere. [...] You can even write well about the moon, even though it's been done over and over. And it will be interesting. You just have to see something in the moon that is your own, not something that others have worked into the ground. "And how is that not a story idea?" he pointed out onto the street, where dawn was already starting to break. "Look over there: there's a monk out walking with a cup, collecting donations for a bell ... Don't you feel a good theme just springing up all by itself? ... There's something tragic here—a black-robed monk in the pale dawn...

Chekhov carried a notebook in which he would jot down impressions, ideas, mini-situations, and pithy phrases. Unlike a writer like Tolstoy, for example, whose extensive, life-long diaries contributed intimately to and interacted with his fictional works, Chekhov's notebook and occasional diary entries are sporadic and minimalistic, written, as it were, on the run. But they capture something essential; these scraps of words would serve as the kernel from which stories would grow. Some of Chekhov's stories can be traced back to these snippets; more often the reader gets a tantalizing glimpse into potential stories that were never written—like fish that he tossed back.

The circumstances of his travel, along with the limitations of the French-Russian postal service during his convalescence in Nice in the fall of 1897, led him to write more than usual in his notebook during that time. He jotted down impressions from a visit to a casino:

> October 9. I saw B.'s mother playing roulette. Unpleasant sight.

> November 15. Monte Carlo. I saw how the croupier stole a louis d'or.

Compare Dostoevsky, himself a gambling addict, who wrote an entire novel, (The Gambler), in which the casino serves as a metaphor for hell, and gambling itself is a life-or-death game with fate, and all of it is packaged as an exposé of the evils of Western European secular culture.

Chekhov's undated notebook entries (presented here in Constance Garnett's translations) recall the format of his early comic stories, an entire world in a phrase:

> The French say: "Laid comme un chenille"—as ugly as a caterpillar.

> That sudden and ill-timed love-affair may be compared to this: you take boys somewhere for a walk; the walk is jolly

and interesting–and suddenly one of them gorges himself with oil paint. The character in the play says to every one: "You've got worms." He cures his daughter of the worms, and she turns yellow. A pregnant woman with short arms and a long neck, like a kangaroo. A man, who, to judge from his appearance, loves nothing but sausages and sauerkraut.

His income is twenty-five to fifty thousand, and yet out of poverty he shoots himself.

A government clerk gave his son a thrashing because he had only obtained five marks in all his subjects at school. It seemed to him not good enough. When he was told that he was in the wrong, that five is the highest mark obtainable, he thrashed his son again–out of vexation with himself.

The hen sparrow believes that her cock sparrow is not chirping but singing beautifully.

A large fat barmaid–a cross between a pig and white sturgeon.

Whenever he reads in the newspaper about the death of a great man, he wears mourning.

Z. goes to a doctor, who examines him and finds that he is suffering from heart disease. Z. abruptly changes his way of life, takes medicine, can only talk about his disease; the whole town knows that he has heart disease and all the doctors, whom he regularly consults, say that he has got heart disease. He does not marry, gives up amateur theatricals, does not drink, and when he walks does so slowly and hardly breathes. Eleven years later he has to go to Moscow and there he consults a specialist. The latter finds that his heart is perfectly sound. Z. is overjoyed, but he can no longer return to a normal life, for he has got accustomed to going to bed early and to walking slowly, and he is bored if he cannot speak of his disease. The only result is that he gets to hate doctors–that is all.

The wife cried. The husband took her by the shoulders and shook her, and she stopped crying.

He died from fear of cholera.

A gentleman owns a villa near Mentone; he bought it out of the proceeds of the sale of his estate in the Tula province. I saw him in Kharkhov to which he had come on business; he gambled away the villa at cards and became a railway clerk; after that he died.

The wife writes; the husband does not like her writing, but out of delicacy says nothing and suffers all his life.

An actress, forty years old, ugly, ate a partridge for dinner, and I felt sorry for the partridge, for it occurred to me that in its life it had been more talented, more sensible, and more honest than that actress.

(From Project Guttenberg: http://www.gutenberg.org/files/12494/12494.txt)

In a famous May 10, 1886 letter to his brother Alexander, Chekhov gave advice on how to write a good nature description. One key detail, fished out of the environment, is more effective than any attempt to catalogue all the elements in a scene:

In my opinion, descriptions of nature must be quite short and *à propos*. Commonplaces like "The setting sun, swimming in the waves of the darkening sea, bathed it in scarlet gold" etc., and "Swallows, flying over the surface of the water, chirped merrily"–this kind of commonplace needs to be tossed away. In descriptions of nature one must seize on specific details, assembling them in a particular way so that upon reading them, when you close your eyes, you see a picture. For example, you will get a moonlit night if you write that a bright star gleams in a broken bottle shard on a millpond dam and a plump black shadow of a dog or wolf darts past. Nature comes alive if you do not shrink from comparing its phenomena with human actions.

Chekhov cited this example in the 1886 story "The Wolf"; it also recurs later in *The Seagull*, when the young writer Treplyov characterizes his rival Trigorin's craft:

My description of the moonlit night is long and unnatural. Trigorin has worked out his methods; it's easy for him ... He has the neck of a broken bottle gleaming on the weir, and the millwheel's black shadow—and there's his moonlit night, but what I have is the shimmering light, and the silent twinkling of stars, and the distant sound of a piano, fading away in the quiet fragrant air ... it's agonizing.

Chekhov's descriptions are ruthlessly efficient; not a word is out of place. Their power derives not merely from the writer's ability to choose the precise word for a given artistic purpose; on a deeper level, they fit into his overall artistic sensibility, according to which what is left implicit is far more powerful than what is said or written directly. There is a whole picture behind every word, just as everything we say in life is only the tiniest fragment of the world we live in. Our language is limited; it is a miracle that we ever manage to communicate anything important. This fact reflects a general truth of psychology—an invisible threat is scarier than the scary thing we see before us; or of religion—the divine transcends any ability to capture or describe it in human language. Chekhov's carefully chosen words enable the reader to reconstitute a whole world: the whole lake, not just the broken bottle; the inner life of the fish, even if the outer fish is the only thing we see. According to this principle, everything of importance lies beyond the words. The unfulfilled promise, the marriage proposal that does not come to pass, the justice that is not done, the gun that shoots offstage—all of these elements give Chekhov's plots their power. A character's unspoken thoughts bear her anguish. In "In the Ravine," Lipa sits down by a pond, holding the corpse of her murdered baby. She is alone in the universe with her sorrow. A woman brings her horse to the water, but the horse does not drink. "It won't drink....," comments Lipa. That is all, but that is enough.

What might be called the "world-to-word" relationship is powerful and precise in Chekhov's writing. His fine craftsmanship allows the alert reader to see everything in the picture, in the story, as well as in the world beyond it:

> A bedroom. The moonlight shines through the window so brightly that even the buttons on his night shirt are visible.

As mentioned earlier in this chapter, much of this fine craft emerged from Chekhov's summers, when he wandered the countryside, observing the world around him. It permeates his works from the mid-1880s on. The late story, "The House with the Mezzanine" (1896), reflects, in fictional form, this process. A landscape artist spends the summer painting. He meets a girl, "Misius," with whom he spends long lazy days—neither of them apparently doing any work. During their idle time together, feelings of love begin to develop. By contrast, her elder sister, the socially active Lida, toils from morning to night without rest, in hopes of making the world a better place. They quarrel, and Lida sends her sister away. Summer ends, and nothing is left of the romance, only "The Artist's Story"—which is, in fact, the story's subtitle. "The House with the Mezzanine" serves as an allegory for the creation of a work of art from the interaction between the artist's idleness, which renders him receptive to nature, inspiration, emotion, and love, and the hard work of writing or painting necessary to transform the inspiration into a story or picture when the moment of inspiration has passed.

An "inspirational" friendship

Chekhov always loved and appreciated nature, but the catalyst for his distinctive poetic merging of character into the natural setting may very well have been his close and enduring friendship with Levitan. They were born in the same year (1860), were extremely close, and spent hours and days together in the city as well as the country. Their personal relationships were intricately intertwined: they shared friends, both male and female. At one point Levitan proposed marriage to Chekhov's sister Masha. Like Chekhov, Levitan was extremely attractive to women, and Levitan's extant side of their correspondence betrays a frankness in referring to sexual matters that one can deduce also characterized Chekhov's lost letters to Levitan. Levitan was one of the very few friends with whom Chekhov used the intimate Russian pronoun "ty" ("thee"–the equivalent to the French singular "tu"). As a medical man, Chekhov was well aware of the seriousness of Levitan's heart condition, not to mention the signs of an illness that was possibly syphilis. In addition to his physical ailments, Levitan suffered crippling bouts of depression that led to at least one suicide attempt that brought Chekhov rushing to his side.

Like many artists of his generation, Levitan spent the summers painting outside in nature. Meanwhile, Anton's brother and Levitan's classmate Nikolai, having dropped out of art school, went into hiding to avoid the draft and prowled the most disreputable districts of Moscow, sponging off acquaintances and accepting advances for artwork that he did not complete. Nikolai's behavior enraged family members, colleagues, and friends alike. By contrast, despite his disorderly and chaotic lifestyle, Levitan, like Chekhov, worked intensely on his art during the summers; the two of them spent day after day together, and both of them produced a series of masterpieces drawing on their observations of the embeddedness of human life within nature.

Their genres were different but complementary. Both of them

came to be identified with an aesthetics of "mood" (*nastroenie* in Russian). Chekhov's works feature plots dominated by a progression of emotional states. And Levitan's paintings—he focused almost exclusively on non-urban spaces—spiritualize nature and convey the essence of the human soul. Notably, on his most famous canvases, Levitan did not paint people, though his landscapes usually contain a trace of human influence—a road, a bridge, a church, or other building. Chekhov's brother Nikolai—before he went off the rails—had been known to add a human figure to Levitan's work, for example, the woman in black in the famous 1879 painting *Autumn Day: Sokolniki*. Anton took the next step in this process. Beginning with the summers in Babkino, especially in 1885 when Levitan was close by, Chekhov began to integrate landscape and nature description into his stories, not just as a backdrop, but as a fully active participant in the life of the text. Like his brother, he incorporated the human element; but unlike his brother, he probed beneath the visual surface to the inner life of the individual's soul, linking it to the greater soul of the natural world in which it is embedded. His relationship with Levitan must, at least in part, be credited for this development in his writing.

"The Huntsman," written in Babkino in 1885, exemplifies this sensibility. It fits the "snake who swallowed the egg" pattern—first a scene is set: a field of rye on a hot summer day—not a sign of life. "The scorched grass looks mournfully, devoid of hope: though there will be rain, it will never be green." The figure of a man appears in the distance, crossing the field. Suddenly his name, Yegor Vlasych, is called; as he approaches, a woman appears "as though she had grown up out of the earth." They have a brief conversation, in which the reader learns that though they had gotten married 12 years ago, the man had been drunk at the time and he felt that he had been coerced into the marriage. They have never lived together as a couple; the man had left his bride immediately after the wedding to live in the landowner's mansion and serve as his huntsman. The abandoned wife, Pelagea, has been yearning for him ever since; instead of raising a family of her own, she takes in orphans to nurse with a bottle. She timidly begs him to come back to her, but he proclaims his independence and his primeval nature as a hunter–a predator who must kill. He then proceeds on his way, leaving her and the field in their initial state. At the end of the story, Pelagea whispers, "Goodbye, Yegor Vlasych!" and rises onto her tiptoes, to see his white cap at least one more time. The story is simple, yet exquisitely balanced between opposing forces: male-female; killer-nurturer; forest-field–to a degree that the human beings are even an afterthought. It conveys an extraordinary sense of longing and sadness, through Chekhov's incorporation of the natural world seamlessly into the heroine's spiritual and emotional life. All nouns in the Russian language, as in Romance languages, carry an attribute of gender: masculine, feminine, or, in Slavic languages, neuter–not just people and animals, but inanimate objects, too. And the Russian pronouns convey this gendered identity of everything in the world. So, for example, grass is feminine. The story's first paragraph lacks a human element, but every word is infused with the as-yet invisible heroine's longing (the grass is scorched, mournful, devoid of hope. There is no rain, and the whole world is dying of thirst). The abandoned wife rises from the very earth, of a piece with it, parched too–barren, with no baby of her own to nurse. When the husband leaves, she merges again with the field, unslaked like the grass, and her whispered goodbye at the story's end could very well be no more than a faint puff of air. This famous story would serve as a turning point in Chekhov's development from a writer for the "small press" to a major figure in Russian literature. In future stories, Chekhov continued to develop this seamless merging of human being with the natural environment.

"The Grasshopper"

Levitan and Chekhov's intimate friendship continued for several years, but it was to be interrupted by a serious falling out in 1892. We will jump ahead in time to take a close look at this incident, and a famous story that Chekhov wrote about it using the "summer in the country" frame. Chekhov had spent the summer of 1891 in relative isolation, while Levitan stayed at a different gentry estate, near where Chekhov's on-again, off-again girlfriend Lika Mizinova was living for the summer. There, the artist conducted a lively social life, including with Lika and with his own mistress for the summer, a married woman and dilettante named Sofia Kuvshinnikova. Chekhov published a story, "The Grasshopper" (or "Flibbertigibbet"), quite transparently telling the story of this affair. The scandalous real-life connections surrounding the tale may unfortunately distract from its remarkable literary qualities as one of the best examples of Chekhov's treatment of character and nature, so we'll take this opportunity to examine it in depth. Whereas "The Huntsman" gives only the characters and the landscape, "The Grasshopper" adds in the figure of the artist (the lover), in pointed contrast to the scientist (the long-suffering husband). Not coincidentally, the artist and the scientist may represent Levitan and Chekhov; alternatively, they may represent the two competing sides of Chekhov himself. The woman, though easily recognizable as Kuvshinnikova, bears traces of Lika Mizinova.

The famous fable of the ant and the grasshopper (the ant toils all summer; the grasshopper wastes the summer singing) serves as the story's subtext. The scientist (the ant) is the cuckolded husband, a hard-working doctor, Osip. The artist (the grasshopper) is Ryabovsky, unsurprisingly, a landscape painter. The story's heroine, Olga (like her prototype), has decorated her city home with Bohemian pretensions, like an artist's studio; in her living room she hangs sketches (her own and others') on the walls, sets up easels, and strews picturesque objects around—Chinese parasols, colorful pieces of cloth, and daggers; another room is decorated with artifacts from peasant life: woven rope sandals, scythes, a pitchfork, and primitive popular prints. Like her prototype, she fancies herself an artist and wants to be associated with a genius.

She tags along with Ryabovsky and a group of other painters who have gone out to the river Volga, like the "Wanderers" or "Itinerants" who focused on subjects from Russian life. Olga and Ryabovsky have an affair, which ends at the end of the summer. Meanwhile Osip—unconcerned for his own welfare, probably because of his wife's abandonment of him—contracts diphtheria after a selfless (or self-destructive) effort to save a child suffering from the disease. As her husband lies dying, Olga learns that it was he, so self-effacing and modest, not the flashy artist, who was the true genius. Thus, the story follows the plot path of the unexpected ending, which in Chekhov's early, anecdotal stories serve as a comic punchline. In "The Grasshopper," though, it bears a tragic tonality, deriving partly from its autobiographical resonances, and partly from its allegorical message about the nature of science and art.

As in a play, the story takes the reader through a series of settings: the site of Olga's wedding, where the artist likens her in her wedding dress to a supple cherry tree; her apartment with its artsy decor; Olga's dacha and the rough huts where the artists live and work on the Volga; a boat on the river; the artist's studio; and, finally, her own home in the city—where her husband will die. Clothing and exterior appearance are a theme throughout; at one point, in an echo of the opening scene, Olga conjures up a picturesque scene after a peasant wedding she plans to attend the next day: "a grove, birds singing, spots of sunlight on the grass, and all of us are various-colored spots against a bright green background—so original, in the French expressionist taste." And she sends her husband—exhausted from his hard labor earning money to support her lifestyle – back to the city to get her the perfect dress. What is remarkable about Chekhov's scene construction in the story is that he inverted the elements, repeating them from one scene to the next. So, the dining room's contrived peasant décor migrates out to the artists' huts on the riverbank, now real. And when Olga visits Ryabovsky's studio in the city after their relationship has ended, she brings him a still life study she has done—a *nature morte* (literally, "dead nature"). The woman who has replaced her as the artist's latest lover is hiding behind a painting in the studio—a new source of inspiration for the artist to replace the one (Olga) he has used up.

In the scene on the boat, it is September, and the bright summer landscape has turned gray and cold. Ryabovsky, already bored with Olga and depressed (like his prototype), gazes gloomily at the river, "and it seemed that nature had stripped from the Volga the luxuriant green carpets of the banks, the diamond-like reflections of the sun's rays, the transparent blue distance, and had packed it all away in trunks until next spring, and ravens flew over the Volga, teasing it, 'Naked! Naked!'" Here Chekhov applied the gendered language technique he had used in "The Huntsman," adding in some poetic sound play. The Volga (like the word for river "*reka*") is feminine in gender, so the phrase "teasing it" can also be translated, "teasing her." Furthermore, long "o" sounds dominate: ravens ("*vorony*"), as in the heroine's name, which they are cawing out loud. And Olga, the Volga, and the word "naked" (*golaya*) also echo each other in the text. So Olga, like the river, has been stripped of her gaudy exterior through the artist's "use" of her (and the Volga) for his art. And she is naked morally as well: as for the fine clothing that her husband had toiled his life away to buy for her, Korostelev, her husband's colleague who is attending him during his dying hours, blames her for the loss of this brilliant scientist:

> He worked like an ox, day and night, no one spared him, and a young scholar, future professor, had to seek patients and do translations at night to pay for these .... miserable rags!' Korostelev looked with hatred at Olga Ivanovna, seized the sheet with both hands and tore it angrily, as though it [she] was to blame.

The sheet is feminine-gendered in Russian as well, so, as before, "it" can be translated "her." The reader feels the moral message of Olga's guilt, though Chekhov never made it explicit.

Even as he took revenge on Levitan in this story, Chekhov drew upon the potent artistic dialogue he conducted with his friend as they spent the summers together, developing the techniques that would produce Russia's greatest masterpieces, in both landscape painting and the short story. The astonishing combination of artistic techniques manifest in this story—its merging of the human being with the landscape, allegorical treatment of art and science, clever plot reversal at the end, manipulation of the gendered features of the Russian language, and poetic sound play, not to mention its embedded moral message—is not limited to "The Grasshopper," but also pervades Chekhov's mature work. And it all began during Chekhov's summers in the country in the 1880s.

The Steppe

Chekhov's most famous nature work is his long prose piece, *The Steppe*, which draws on impressions from his travels through the Russian and Ukrainian steppe. Its publication in 1889 in a prestigious thick journal, *The Northern Herald*, signaled Chekhov's stature as a writer. Though drawing on the prose-poem style of some works by Turgenev, and Gogol stories, including parts of *Dead Souls*, *The Steppe* was something completely new and original, and was greeted with ecstatic praise by discerning readers. The work is structured through the trope of journey, as a kind of picaresque of the earth's rotation, where the human travelers merge with the landscape and share the spirit of the steppe. A young boy, Yegorushka, leaves home to attend school in the city, far away from the small town where he has lived up to that point with his widowed mother. His uncle and a priest accompany him for the beginning of the long journey. Before long they leave to take care of some business, entrusting the boy to the care of a group of peasants, who are driving a caravan of carts piled high with bales of wool. From a lofty vantage point atop the bales on one of the carts, Yegorushka and the reader can see farther than any other human being; periodically he descends and gets micro-closeups of the flora and fauna, including the peasant cart drivers themselves. At the story's climax, the wagons proceed through a terrifying thunderstorm, during which the boy's high perch is a disadvantage; he is soaked through and falls ill. Ultimately, he arrives safe and sound in the city, where his uncle arranges for his lodging and enrollment into the high school where he is to study in the fall.

Readers seeking a plotline will be disappointed; the story's meaning lies in the majestic and comprehensive panorama it offers of the steppe, complete with close-ups of the living creatures who dwell there. Readers can access deeper meanings by generalizing from the characters and settings in The Steppe to all humanity, and the world itself: depending on how far you pan back, the character is a boy, a Russian (or Ukrainian), or a human being like all of us; the steppe is the steppe, Russia (or Ukraine), or the whole world. Little Yegorushka is dwarfed by the majesty of nature that surrounds him, and as such he is no different from his fellow human beings. The steppe is our world, the cosmos that arouses our wonder but never allows us to understand its deeper secrets. The people surrounding Yegorushka represent various human types, yet each one is an utterly unique individual. From his high perch, Yegorushka and the reader witness the full range of human behavior. One peasant, named Dymov, brutally beats a snake to death, teases and terrifies Yegorushka, and insults the other cart drivers; together with the stories of murder in the steppe Dymov is recounting, the boy and the reader get a sense of not just the steppe, but an entire world, steeped in primordial violence—man against man, man against beast. Dymov cruelly mocks one of the other drivers, and Yegorushka finally gets the courage to scream at him, "In the next world you will burn in hell!" Furious and helpless, he cries out for the bully to be punished: "Beat him! Beat him!" The boy's outburst coincides with the onset of the storm—a storm outside and a storm within—exemplifying Chekhov's distinctive blurring of the boundaries between human being and environment. All four elements unleash their mighty power (earth: the steppe itself; water: the terrifying downpour; air: gale-force wind; fire: the blinding lightning), and danger fills the cosmos, transcending and dwarfing all human capacity for evil. The boy's shout, together with Dymov's own inner turmoil, the emotions, and experiences of the other peasants, has conjured up a scene of the Last Judgment. And as is always the case with Chekhov, there is no answer to the question, "Who is to blame?"

Yegorushka mother's name is Knyazev, from the Russian word for "prince," and his uncle is a wealthy businessman with no children of his own; we deduce that Yegorushka is his heir. So even as the boy enters the city to get an education, he will implicitly be taking on a responsibility to care for the steppe and all of its creatures. Yegorushka's trip sets him on the path from ignorance and innocence to knowledge. From the narrator's references to the progress of the sun across the sky, it is clear that the journey proceeds from East to West (or, as some readers deduce, from Taganrog to Kiev), exemplifying Russia's own fraught historical path (the 19th-century national identity crisis fought out between Westernizers and Slavophiles over the extent of Western influence in Russia). Yegorushka travels during the summer, which, as in Chekhov's own life, is a time for taking in impressions, for communing with nature, until summer ends and the traveler enters the city. There he will put childish things away and begin a life of work and study.

In all these ways, The Steppe raises the most serious questions of human life—our place in the universe, the problem of evil, the transition from innocence to knowledge, Russia's identity, and many more. And yet its most powerful message is musical. The Steppe is best read through the ears; it is closest not to other works of literature, but to a composition very much like Beethoven's Pastoral Symphony. Squint, silence the flailings of your rational mind, and listen.

Take, for example, the narrator's long, lyrical meditation to the steppe in Chapter IV. Just before Yegorushka's uncle and the priest turn him over to the cart drivers, the boy falls into a drowsy reverie and gradually falls asleep, mulling over his impressions of the flat grassland he passes. Several long paragraphs ensue, rich with detail about the life of the steppe. As in Chekhov's most profound works, the landscape becomes infused with a universally human sense of sublime beauty and longing–which we share with all creatures who dwell there–and the music enters a final crescendo. With the exception of the "she" and "her" (which could be "it") referring to the steppe, there are no pronouns in the passage–the verbs come with no subject. The reader is not distinguishing between the emotions and perceptions of the boy, the narrator, the author, even the reader (you and I), and, most importantly, the steppe itself. To give a sense for how this works, I bracket out the "you":

> [...] in everything that [you] see and hear can be felt the triumph of beauty, youth, the flourishing of strength and a passionate thirst for life; the soul resonates with its beautiful, stern homeland, and [you] feel a desire to sour above the steppe together with the night bird. And in this triumph of beauty, in this excess of happiness [you] feel a sense of strain and anguish, as though the steppe knows how alone she is, that her wealth and inspiration perish for the world, in vain, unsung by anyone, unneeded by anyone, and through the joyous clamor [you] hear her yearning, hopeless summons, calling out for a singer! A singer!

One of Chekhov's friends from his university days, Grigory Rossolimo, recalled a conversation with the writer about rhythm and style. Chekhov was especially attentive to phonetics and musicality when constructing endings to a sentence, paragraph, or story. The last word in this long passage in the original Russian is "singer" (*pevtsa*), or "bard," that is, someone who can take all this and put it into words and music, and it is repeated (twice)–though since this word order and the repetition is not always retained by translators, the fact may go unnoticed. At this precise moment, when the music climaxes in the steppe's passionate call for a poet, Yegorushka awakens; his uncle has met up with the wagon train and is talking with one of the peasants. It is never completely safe to identify a literary character with the author, but this scene lends itself to an autobiographical reading. Chekhov, like his little hero, traveled westward through the steppe from a provincial town to the big city, leaving his childhood behind and seeking an education. Yegorushka's observations are Chekhov's; scholars have linked many details in *The Steppe* to the author's experiences of traveling through the steppe, both in his teen years, and in the 1880s. The story was written during a time when he felt the great weight of readers' expectations for this work, which everyone knew would be longer than his previous pieces, and would be published in a major journal. Chekhov's little hero is semi-consciously mulling over the many impressions he has taken in. He is "idle" but when summer ends, he will work, will get his education, and will write—both the boy and the writer he is to become. The call for a singer awakens him; does it come from inside, or from the very steppe?

The Chekhovs had spent the summer of 1888 in a dacha rented at Luka, the Lintvaryovs' estate near the Ukrainian town of Sumy on the Psiol River. Here they developed a lasting friendship with this remarkable gentry family of five siblings, all liberal activists. Two of the daughters were doctors—the eldest blind and suffering from incurable brain cancer; the elder son was a radical under house arrest, and the younger a musician. By 1888, Chekhov had become a famous writer with contacts in the higher reaches of the publishing world. Many of his colleagues and friends came to visit the family in Sumy, which became a lively cultural hub for the summer. They returned in 1889 for one more summer before Chekhov left this stage in his life's path, and the 1880s, behind.

By 1889, Nikolai's erratic lifestyle and his tuberculosis had finally caught up with him. The family took him to Sumy, where he died in mid-June, plunging them into grief. And the theme of death—not the keeling over of a comic clerk, but the deep existential reality of it, entered Chekhov's writing.

4. Petersburg and Literary Fame

Chekhov's artistic trajectory, which began with the "small press," differed from the path taken by the great Russian novelists Turgenev, Dostoevsky, and Tolstoy, whose works were first published in the prestigious thick journals. In all cases, though, it was generally after their initial periodical publication that works would come out in separate editions, in book form. Chekhov published several book-length story collections between 1884 and 1890: *Tales of Melpomene* (1884), *Motley Stories* (1886), *In the Twilight* (1887), and *Gloomy Stories* (1890), primarily as a way to earn income. It was through his ongoing contributions to journals that he honed his craft and expanded his thematic range. To trace these developments, we zig-zag back to pick up events of Chekhov's life during the mid-1880s between his summers in the country. In this chapter, our focus will be on the literary institutions and people in St. Petersburg, which became increasingly important to Chekhov as his fame grew.

The prestigious journals and publishers were based in St. Petersburg, the capital of Russia during Chekhov's lifetime. "The Huntsman" drew attention in these circles when it came out in *St. Petersburg Newspaper* in 1885. During the early 1880s, Chekhov had become a regular contributor of short fiction, as well as a set of journalistic pieces called "Fragments of Moscow Life," to a St. Petersburg weekly called *Fragments*. In December of 1885, at the invitation of its publisher Nikolai Leikin, Chekhov traveled to the capital for the first time. It was during this visit that he became acquainted with famous literary figures who were to become his mentors: Alexei Suvorin, the publisher of the right-leaning nationalist newspaper *New Time* and Dmitry Grigorovich, a prose writer who 40 years earlier had been instrumental in the debut of the then-unknown Fyodor Dostoevsky. Chekhov also gained a mentor and friend in the elderly poet Alexei Pleshcheev, himself famous for his association with Dostoevsky; the two of them had been arrested together in 1849 for involvement in the utopian-socialist revolutionary Petrashevsky Circle. Both Dostoevsky and Pleshcheev had been sentenced to death and brought before a firing squad in December of that year before a courier from the tsar galloped up with a last-minute reprieve and commutation to Siberian prison and exile. With these new acquaintances, Chekhov's literary apprenticeship was over. Suvorin in particular would become one of his closest friends; Chekhov became close to his whole family, during a time when they suffered terrible losses—including the deaths of two of Suvorin's sons and of Chekhov's brother Nikolai. He would stay with Suvorin both in St. Petersburg and at his estate in Feodosia on the Black Sea; they traveled together, including to Europe, and collaborated on various projects, including theatrical productions. Through it all, they conducted an extraordinary correspondence, of which Suvorin's side is available only secondhand, in memoirs by contemporaries and in his own diary entries.

Chekhov began publishing in Suvorin's *New Time* at the end of the 1880s. Stories like "The Kiss" and "Kashtanka" attracted a broad readership, along with works published elsewhere during this time. "The Kiss" is about a nebbish, low-ranking artillery officer who is kissed in the dark by an unknown woman at a party. Though the incident was clearly a case of mistaken identity, the officer's life is changed forever. Importantly, nothing changes on the outside, and he cannot communicate to anyone what happened. "Kashtanka" tells the story of a circus dog who recognizes her former owner in the audience. To this day, "Kashtanka" is a favorite of Russian schoolchildren. And "The Kiss" is widely anthologized worldwide. Through the late 1880s, Chekhov would continue to place stories in other journals, and these too added to his fame. Failure of communication, which will be one of Chekhov's master themes throughout his literary career, is at the center of stories like "Vanka" and "Anguish" (both published in 1886). In "Vanka," an orphan boy who has been taken away from his home in the countryside and apprenticed to a shoemaker in the city writes a letter to his grandfather back in the village on Christmas eve, describing his hard life, and pouring out all his loneliness. Not realizing that letters need proper addresses, he writes "To grandfather in the village" on an envelope and drops the letter into a post box. In "Anguish," a cabby whose son has died tells of his grief to the only creature who will listen–his horse. This message about the inability of human language to convey inner experience expresses a universal truth; it also reflects Chekhov's own struggle as a writer. His many stories of "failed communication" often can be read as allegories for the author's vocation.

Chekhov's personal and professional relationships with his new colleagues would be formative both personally and professionally, but he would never be at ease with the publishing establishment. St. Petersburg periodicals existed in a distinct hierarchy based on readership, literary quality, and political stance. The elaborate politics surrounding which writers wrote for which journals complicated personal interactions, as well as the quality and impartiality of literary criticism. The "politically correct" views among the major journals at the time were liberal and even radical, and Chekhov's growing friendship with the conservative Suvorin, along with his decision to publish in Suvorin's New Time, gained him no allies among the literati. It is likely that this raw political factor hindered some critics from recognizing the artistic quality of his works, though it is a sad fact that pioneering artists rarely get the critical acclaim and understanding that they deserve during their lifetime. Jealousy and various personal alliances among St. Petersburg writers and critics also played a role. At one point late in life, Chekhov was out fishing with a young acquaintance, Alexander Serebrov-Tikhonov, who later recalled that they had witnessed a dog that had caught a fish and tried to devour it alive as the fish beat it on the nose with its tail. Chekhov commented: "Just like our criticism!" The famous proletarian writer Maxim Gorky, with whom

Chekhov became acquainted in the 1890s, recorded a conversation in which Chekhov characterized contemporary literary criticism:

> Critics are like horseflies who keep the horses from plowing. [...] The horse toils, straining all her muscles like strings on a double bass, and a horsefly lands on her rump, and tickles and buzzes. She has to shudder her skin and flap her tail. What is he buzzing about? He hardly understands himself. It's just that he has a restless character and wants to express himself: "I too walk the earth! See? I can even make buzzing noises, I can buzz about everything!" I've been reading criticism of my stories for twenty-five years, and I cannot recall a single point of any value, I have not heard even one good piece of advice. Except for one time when Skabichevsky made an impression on me; he wrote that I would die drunk under a fence...

In any case, even as he published in the major St. Petersburg journals, Chekhov was and would remain a Moscow writer. Though he would often travel to the capital, primarily in connection with publishing and theatrical productions, his home was in Moscow, and, between 1892 and 1897, at his estate of Melikhovo outside the city.

Readers of Chekhov's letters can be grateful that he stayed in Moscow, for it is to Suvorin, Grigorovich, Pleshcheev, and other St. Petersburg correspondents that Chekhov wrote some of his most memorable letters. He was a sociable creature who needed an interlocutor, and did not express his philosophical, ethical, or political views in monologic fashion. It is tantalizing to try to imagine Chekhov's conversations with his closest friends—his tone of voice and listening style, and of course the things he never wrote down. The tone and subject matter of these conversations leave their mark on the letters in which they continued their dialogues. To judge from extant letters, frank and bawdy elements abounded in his conversations with close male friends like Franz Schekhtel, Kiselyov, and Levitan—not to mention his elder brothers. More tantalizing are the long intimate discussions of life, art, and the political realities of the time that Chekhov had with his close friends–their content and tone lost forever. What we do have is his letters, which carried on the dialogue when the friends were separated. These letters are precious not only for the ideas he expressed in them, but also for insights into his biography and creative process. Some story ideas, and particularly phrasing, emerge in epistolary conversations; passages, scenes, or images from his letters often recur in his fiction and drama. If Chekhov's early extant letters are fascinating for what they tell us about his relationships with family and intimate friends and about his early years in Taganrog and Moscow, as well as about his developing personal ethical views and moral code, the letters written from the mid-1880s on show a new depth and thoughtfulness that came with his maturity and his clear sense of his stance as a writer.

This new phase in Chekhov's career can be dated to March 25, 1886, when Dmitry Grigorovich wrote him a letter from St. Petersburg. It turned out that Grigorovich had been following his work closely, and had recommended his stories to Suvorin and to others in the literary establishment. In his letter Grigorovich reported that they all agreed that Chekhov had "real talent," far beyond that of his generation of writers:

> [...] You, I am sure, have been called to write several superb, truly artistic works. You will commit a great moral sin if you do not justify these expectations. Here is what is necessary for that: respect for talent, which is given so rarely. Give up writing for deadlines. I don't know your material situation; if you lack funds, it is better to starve, as we did in our time. Save your impressions for carefully conceived and polished work [...]. One such work will be a hundred times more valued than a hundred fine stories scattered at various times to newspapers; you will immediately win a prize and will be brought to the attention of discerning people and then of the entire reading public.

Grigorovich cautioned Chekhov to avoid "cynicism," prurience, and cheap tricks, then urged him to sign his upcoming book (*Motley Tales*) with his real name.

This letter from a famous writer struck Chekhov like a "bolt of lightning," like "an order from the governor to 'leave town within 24 hours!'" and he responded immediately, on March 28, expressing deep emotion and gratitude:

> If I have a gift that needs to be respected, then, I repent before the purity of your heart, up until now I have not respected it. [...] I have hundreds of acquaintances in Moscow, including a couple dozen writers, and I cannot think of even one who would read me or would see me as an artist. There is a so-called "literary circle" in Moscow: talented and ordinary writers of all ages and types get together once a week in a room in a Moscow restaurant and wag their tongues. If I were to go there and read even a small part of your letter, they would laugh in my face.

The second reason Chekhov gave for not respecting his literary activity was professional: he was a doctor, "up to [his] ears" in his medical practice, never spending more than a single day on any of his stories. He claimed that up to that time he had written "mechanically, semiconsciously, with no concern whatsoever about the reader, or about myself ... I wrote and tried in every way not to waste on a story images and pictures that were dear to me, and which I, God knows why, cherished and carefully stashed away." In the city, he noted, it was impossible for him to devote much time to anything of length, but he promised his correspondent that he would write something serious during the summer.

The effect of Grigorovich's letter, and of the support and encouragement Chekhov received from other luminaries in the literary world, cannot be underestimated, though it is true that the originality and sheer quality of his writing were destined to earn recognition sooner or later. A major landmark came in 1888 when he was awarded the prestigious Pushkin Prize for his collection *In* the *Twilight*, sharing it with the prominent prose writer Vladimir Korolenko. With this recognition came higher expectations of readers and critics, including pressure to write a novel in the tradition of the great Russian classics. The pressure was internal as well, and during this period Chekhov began to refer to his "novel," a work he claimed was well underway, consisting of several stories linked by shared characters, intrigue, and ideas. It was never clear to what work he might have been referring, though manuscripts such as "After the Theater," "At the Zelenins'," and "A Letter," have been identified as possible constituent parts. Ultimately, Chekhov, the author of sublime long stories like *My Life* (1896), "Ward No. 6" (1892), and *Three Years* (1895), would never write a "loose baggy monster" Russian novel like those of Dostoevsky and Tolstoy. In his early years, the strict parameters of the "small press" for which he wrote precluded lengthy treatment of any theme. And the habits of economical craftsmanship he developed in response to these requirements stayed with him throughout all his subsequent writing. But beginning in the late 1880s, Chekhov fully intended to write something long and serious. *The Steppe* is the most notable product of this impulse, and as we shall soon see, it has been interpreted as one component part in a set of three stories that add up to something like a distinctively Chekhovian novel. Any remaining novelistic impulse during the late 1880s may have been deflected into his writing for the theater, for example, his 1889 play *The Wood Demon*.

Astonishing productivity

Whatever the length and genre of his individual works, Chekhov's overall productivity was astonishing. The academic collection of his collected works comprises 30 volumes—no more or less than Dostoevsky's. Chekhov's characters come from all social groups and represent all the professions, from the rural peasantry to the landowning nobility, and everything in between: students, actors, the bohemian underclass, professors, convicts, "kept women," bourgeois wives, writers, the intelligentsia, teachers, factory owners, peasants, government employees, military soldiers and officers, cabbies, waiters ... the list goes on and on. Though he never wrote a novel, and though he lived only 44 years–in comparison to Dostoevsky's 60, Turgenev's 64, and Tolstoy's 82, Chekhov actually surpassed his famous predecessors in range and reach.

Although by 1888 Chekhov had clearly entered the literary elite, he still hesitated to commit himself fully to fiction writing. Grigorovich's admonition to give up pseudonyms echoed Suvorin's request that Chekhov sign his real name to his contributions to *New Time*. He agreed only reluctantly. His decision to sign his works for Suvorin with his name represented a major turning point in his career, a new commitment to his "mistress" (literature) at the expense of his "wife" (medicine). He had been saving his name for serious work, which for him meant research and writing in the area of science and medicine. Chekhov was a creature of his age, a committed empiricist and Darwinist for whom biology lay at the heart of history and human behavior. Throughout the 1880s and even most of the 90s, he cherished the dream of doing scholarly work and ultimately earning a doctorate and an academic position. Early on, while still a medical student, he had proposed to his brother Alexander (not jokingly) that they write a "History of Sexual Dominance" together. Nothing came of this research project, though the theme pervaded Chekhov's works from beginning to end. Toward the end of the 1880s, Chekhov also turned his attention to another key subject for research, mental illness. In 1887, he assisted Pyotr Arkhangelsky, one of the doctors he had practiced under during his medical apprenticeship in Voskresensk, in a study of Russia's psychiatric institutions. This theme would also spill over into his fiction and dramatic writing. Later, his academic interests turned to statistics and demographics; public health and prisons were also abiding concerns. So this commitment to fiction writing represented a key milepost in his life.

Chekhov's desire to make his mark as a scholar would lead to his trip to the prison colony on Sakhalin Island in 1890 and his demographic research on the population there, published in his book, *Sakhalin Island*, in 1891-3. Ultimately he would become, briefly, an "academic," though not in a scientific field, when he was named an honorary academician in literature by the Russian Academy of Sciences in 1900; however, within two years he would give up this title in protest against the Emperor's rejection of Maxim Gorky's selection into the Academy. Readers of Chekhov's short stories can be grateful for his abiding interest in the medical and physiological side of moral issues, and his desire to make his mark as a scholar. He channeled his trademark "objectivity" as a scientist in new ways into the works he wrote beginning in the late 1880s. His scientific knowledge, commitment to objective facts and firm empirical stance—not to mention his day-by-day work as a healer—gave weight and authority to his treatment of momentous themes like sexuality, mental illness, and death, and ensure that his depiction of the human experience feels contemporary, tangible, and true over a hundred years later.

Some of Chekhov's most famous works reflect his interest in mental illness and abnormal mental states. Two extraordinary stories of the late 1880s, "Sleepy" (1888) and "An Attack of Nerves" (1888), express a powerful sense of psychological distress, conveyed from inside his protagonists' consciousnesses, and contextualized in a rich depiction of their immediate environment. In these stories, moral questions are fully entangled in the characters' emotional and psychological life. In "Sleepy," a 13-year-old girl, Varka, is performing slave labor in a shoemaker's household. She has been entrusted with caring for a colicky baby, whose screaming will not let her sleep. Kept awake at night, beaten, and forced to do household tasks during the day, the little nanny begins to hallucinate. The reader is fully inside Varka's consciousness, looking out through her eyes. At the moment her disturbed mind identifies the baby as the "enemy" causing all her misery, she smothers it—an act conveyed in passing, via the Russian equivalent of a subordinate clause—and falls into a blissful sleep. The hallucinations that come to Varka are not only a fantasy and symptom of her abnormal state; they also tell her own back story, recounting her father's death, which was undoubtedly the precipitating factor that led to her enslavement in this stranger's household. The visions are triggered by the flickering of the green icon lamp in the shoemaker's home and by the sounds of the baby's crying. Varka sings the Russian lullaby refrain "Bayushki-bayou," and in these sounds, her memory's ear catches the "boo-boo-boo" sound her father made when he suffered his fatal internal "rupture." These seemingly nonsense syllables bear a deeper inner logic; their message is musical in nature and conveys a depth of human suffering inaccessible to ordinary forms of cognition. Unspoken in the story is the murderess's inevitable sentencing to prison and exile in Siberia—itself to become a preoccupation of the author within a year after he completed "Sleepy." Anyone interested in appreciating the depths of Chekhov's poetic art in this story—reflected quite well in nearly all English translations—should compare it to Katherine Mansfield's baldly plagiarized and inferior 1910 version, "The Child who Was Tired."

"An Attack of Nerves" was written for a collection in honor of the brilliant young writer Vsevolod Garshin, who suffered severe depression, threw himself down a Moscow stairwell, and died from his injuries in 1887 at the age of 33. The hero of the story is a sensitive law student named Vasiliev. Two friends, whose academic fields of study—art and medicine—bear near-allegorical import, convince him to join them on an outing one winter night to Moscow's brothel district; though they have been frequent clients, this is his first time. The three proceed from one establishment to the next. Vasiliev, who has been expecting something exotic, dark, and mysterious, is shocked by the banality and routine nature of the brothels, and flees into the cold night. Channeling a message that is Tolstoyan and Dostoevskian at the same time, he thinks in agony:

> It's either one thing or the other: either it only seems to us
> that prostitution is an evil, and we are exaggerating, or, if

prostitution is in fact as evil as it is assumed to be, then these dear friends of mine are just the same slaveowners, rapists and murderers as those inhabitants of Syria and Cairo who are depicted in *The Cornfield*. Now they are singing, laughing, sharing clever thoughts, but aren't they the ones who are at this very moment exploiting hunger, ignorance, and stupidity? They—and I was their witness. What place is there here for their humanity, medicine, and art?"

Overwhelmed by his experience and his inability to reconcile what he has witnessed with his moral convictions, Vasiliev falls into dark despair, prompting his friends to take him to a psychiatrist, who examines and interviews him, and sends him off with some medicine. At the end of the story, the reader learns that Vasiliev is prone to attacks just like this one; he feels ashamed of his behavior—he's "experienced it all before"—and the psychiatrist had known about his case before he met him. In this way, Chekhov undermines the reader's initial impression that the story is primarily an attack on the institution of prostitution—though indeed it is that. But it is other things as well: an examination, from inside, of the psychological and emotional experience of a nervous breakdown; a contribution to a literary conversation with other 19th-century Russian writers who had addressed the subject of prostitution (for example, Gogol, "Nevsky Prospect" [1835] and Dostoevsky, *Notes from Underground* [1864]); and a probing examination of the problems of action and conscience that were so central to Russian literature of the time—a complex mix of psychological, philosophical, and political powerlessness that inflicts a character type called "the superfluous man." For his part, Tolstoy is reported to have detected a "false note" in the story and claimed that "the hero should have first 'used' [the prostitute] and only afterwards tormented himself." Indeed, Vasiliev takes no action whatsoever; he flees the brothel without either to "using" or helping an abused prostitute—unlike his friend the art student, who later gets into a fight trying to protect a girl who'd been beaten, and is thrown (uncoincidentally) down the front stairs. In other words, Vasiliev suffers something that we could daringly call "impotence," both the usual and the ethical kind—passivity in the face of evil. Despite his soul-searching, he is no less guilty than his companions.

"Improvisation on a root"

As in all his mature stories, Chekhov manipulated the setting to convey a moral drama—both by placing the action of "An Attack of Nerves" in Moscow's well-known brothel district and by framing the story within a snowfall; its whiteness represents a purity that clashes with the sinfulness that Vasiliev witnesses and cannot understand, underlining his own fall from innocence to knowledge. On the poetic level, the story exemplifies a uniquely Chekhovian constructive principle that we can label "improvisation on a root." The Russian language features an intricately structured system of morphology; basic lexical meaning inheres in roots, to which prefixes and suffixes are added to form words that are related both in sound and meaning. This highly regular structure of word-formation contrasts with English, which possesses a rich and diverse vocabulary drawn from a wide variety of world languages, but is not strongly inflected. With its easily rhymed inflectional patterns and relatively limited range of word roots, Russian lends itself to very rich linguistic and structural play based on word structure and other features of the language's complex grammar. Many of Chekhov's works can be seen as emerging in a kind of phonetic and lexical improvisation on the theme inherent in one root. A story takes as a point of origin a word, or word root, and by repeating the root throughout the text in various combinations of prefixes and suffixes, builds a musical, poetic composition. The root meaning is not random, but conveys something of moral importance. "An Attack" builds its improvisation on the Russian root "pad/pav/pal" which refers to "falling. The title in Russian is

"*Pripadok*," an attack or seizure. Garshin, who was at the center of Chekhov's mind when he wrote the story, fell [*padal* or *upal*] down a stairwell. In the strong Russian literary tradition addressing the problem of prostitution, prostitutes are known as "fallen [*padshie*] women"–a phrase that is repeated over and over throughout the story. The action takes place in scenes of the falling snow (*padaet*), which in Vasiliev's mind represents innocence–before it is trampled. So in the scene in Chapter V where, shocked when he sees that a prostitute who has been abused is drunk, he rushes out of the brothel into the falling snow: "Its flakes, falling [*popav*] into the light, lazily circled in the air like fluff, and even more lazily fell [*padali*] onto the earth [...] 'And how can snow fall [*padat'*] in this alley!' thinks Vasiliev." The reader is inside Vasiliev's head, sharing his agonizing thoughts. A passerby, seeing his anguish, grabs him by the shoulders, and kisses his cheek, then stumbles. "Hold on! Don't fall! (*ne padai!*) he shouts, as if to himself. But of course, the warning is addressed, futilely, to Vasiliev. The root "*pad*," then, operates on multiple levels, affecting the reader audially as well as through its immediate denotative meaning. In this story, Chekhov engaged with a social evil with an intensity worthy of the great Russian classics, but ultimately with an irony, sense of artistic balance, lush poetic texture, and empathy that is uniquely his own.

The theme of illness and death

When Chekhov turned to the theme of death in 1889 in "A Boring Story," it was without a trace of irony or distance. This profoundly autobiographical and philosophical work bears an intensity and depth that reflects the many tensions and changes in Chekhov's life during this period. He was approaching 30. He was famous. Several people close to him had died, including his brother Alexander's common-law wife Anna, who passed away from tuberculosis, as well as two of Suvorin's sons–one by suicide and the other from a sudden illness. His brother Nikolai's death in June 1889 came as a shock. Although as a doctor Chekhov had cared for countless dying people, witnessed numerous deaths, and performed many autopsies, this was the first death of someone in his immediate family—a young man, just two years older than himself. Furthermore, the cause of Nikolai's death was tuberculosis, a disease that Chekhov, despite his denials, must have known afflicted him too, for ever since 1884 he had suffered bouts of blood-spitting. Despite continuing his intermittent medical practice, he was now focusing on his writing, which was the source of his fame and of his income. A career in science, which he had long hoped to pursue, was becoming increasingly unlikely. All of these tensions and experiences—his medical knowledge, the new pressures that had come with fame, his personal sorrow, and direct contact with death—poured into this story of a distinguished professor of medicine facing death. The story's original title, "My Name and I," reflects the importance of Chekhov's decision, under pressure from his editors, finally to sign his own name to his literary works. Indeed, the story begins with the professor's sense of alienation from his name, leading to the moment when the reader realizes, with a shock, that this is a first-person narration:

> There is in Russia a distinguished professor, Nikolai Stepanovich such-and-such, bearing the highest rank and a knighthood; he has been awarded so many Russian and foreign honors that when he has to wear them, his students call him "the iconostasis." He has the most aristocratic circle of acquaintances; at least over the last 25-30 years in Russia, there has never been a famous scholar with whom he was not intimately acquainted. [...] He is a member of all the Russian and three foreign universities. And so on and so forth. All of this and much else that could be said, comprises what is called my name.

Chekhov's hero has achieved the highest level of fame possible for a scholar. At 62, he falls ill and experiences an existential crisis that gradually distances him from everything he once cared about: his wife and children, his teaching and academic career, and a foster daughter named Katya, who had at one point run away to join the theater and serves as a shadow muse for the artist he is not. Nikolai Stepanovich's medical knowledge is sufficient for him to realize, as he notes early on, that he has only six months to live. The story takes him and the reader through those six months, moving him gradually through time and space—from winter (the university and the city) to summer (his dacha in the countryside), and ultimately to a distant city—Kharkov in Ukraine—where, after one last, unexpected visit from Katya, who at this key point in the story might be seen as a kind of angel of death, he finds himself alone.

Several famous Chekhov works feature a thunderstorm at a key moment (for example, in Chapter VII of *The Steppe* and Act II of *Uncle Vanya*), reflecting a protagonist's inner crisis, which, though intensely private, is shared with other characters, and with all of nature. In this story, the storm, which the professor identifies with the peasant term "sparrow night," occurs one quiet night at his dacha; unlike the storms in other works, this one takes place inside Nikolai Stepanovich's soul—the night itself is calm and clear. This internal tempest mysteriously affects the others in his family as well—his wife, his daughter, and Katya, all of them, too, awake this night—like a presentiment of death. Outside, though, all is still—"*dead* silence," literally. Readers can calculate the story's timeline from the professor's statement at the outset that he has six months to live, to the end point of that six-month period, in his lonely hotel room in Kharkov (a city occasionally associated with the theme of death in Chekhov's works). The chapters decrease in length as the story progresses. Time and space inexorably compress in on the professor until he has nowhere to go; he must leave the story, and his name behind. His farewell to Katya, then, reads as a farewell not only to her, but also to life itself.

Critics loved the story, at least in part because it engages the "big questions" with a solemnity reminiscent of Dostoevsky and Tolstoy. Readers then and now have seized upon Nikolai Stepanovich's assertion that his only faith is in science; that he has no greater philosophy (no "general idea") as the story's point, to wit: one must have an explicit personal philosophy in order to live a meaningful life. But Chekhov's works, including this one, can never be reduced to a single message or particular philosophy. His art operates holistically, communicating a number of simultaneous "messages," or melodies, on different levels, from material and specific to abstract and emotional: the progress of human relationships; allegories of art and science; a succession of moods; and a development of musical sound textures. In "A Boring Story," all these levels are in play, and in balance.

Family, love, theater; medicine; science—all of it pales against the reality of the body's decay and death. In a letter of 1889 (the year this story was published), Chekhov wrote: "When dissecting a corpse, even the most inveterate spiritualist must necessarily face the question: where here is the soul?" In "A Boring Story" Chekhov probed into the way the human soul is nested in the body. The physical world wraps itself around us, beginning with our bodies and extending out to the remotest connections we make to the physical world. This view of the outside world as an extension of the human being's bodily shell, as scholar Alexander Chudakov called it, is one of Chekhov's artistic trademarks; it culminates in "The Man in a Shell" (1898), in which the metaphor is used to pose profound political, psychological and philosophical questions. What we observe in "A Boring Story" is the process by which a human being sheds his shells, beginning with the most public and external (professional life), and proceeding through the ever-deeper levels of friends, then family, to the point where he must leave the world behind. And despite Chekhov's commitment to science—stated firmly throughout his life, and by the professor in this story—art ultimately has the upper hand.

A unique path in Russian literature

I have gone on at some length about three stories–*The Steppe*, "An Attack of Nerves," and "A Boring Story"–because of their extraordinary power as literature, and because they offer the opportunity to address Chekhov's artistic techniques in them, and for the compelling window they open onto a very important transitional period in the author's life, and because their artistic and autobiographical elements touch on universal human questions. The scholar Marina Senderovich read these three works, taken together, as Chekhov's missing novel–an "existential trilogy" treating three ages of human life: childhood (aesthetics), young adulthood (ethics), and old age (religion). The theme of education and knowledge–reflecting Chekhov's preoccupation with epistemology–permeates all three: a child's departure for school; a young adult's university studies; and an old man's reflection on his life's work as a scholar and scientist. *The Steppe* focuses on the way we leave behind childish things. "An Attack of Nerves" narrates adult choices: vocation, learning, morality. And "A Boring Story" offers an unflinching look at the prospect of death and the process of dying. It could be this autobiographical urgency that gives these stories their extraordinary power, but it is their universal applicability to human life that has kept them alive long after the author's own death at an age that, for a healthy man, would be only the middle of his life's journey.

It is during this period that Chekhov felt Tolstoy's influence most profoundly. "A Boring Story" responds in subtle ways to Tolstoy's famous 1886 "The Death of Ivan Ilyich," one of world literature's starkest and most ruthless explorations of the reality of death. In a letter of 1890 to composer Pyotr Tchaikovsky's brother Modest, Chekhov put Tolstoy first on his list of the greatest Russian artists (Tchaikovsky took second place and the painter Ilya Repin third). Chekhov had a deep and abiding respect for Tolstoy, whom he would meet in 1895. The Tolstoyan influence extends well beyond their shared theme of death in these two stories. Beginning in the mid-1880s, many of Chekhov's works respond to Tolstoy's treatment of sexuality and infidelity. Tolstoy's *Anna Karenina* is the inevitable reference point for many of these stories, from "A Misfortune" (1886) to "About Love" (1898), and "The Lady with the Dog" (1899). Some of Chekhov's early pieces for Suvorin feature what some contemporaries, including Grigorovich, would call a "cynical" treatment of female sexuality, but, following advice from his mentors, or his own inner compass, soon he applied a broader humanism to the subject. Tolstoy's influence is key to this change. The long 1888 story, "The Name-Day Party," in which a pregnant wife loses her baby after a day of superficial social interactions, engages with Tolstoy's theme of insincerity in human relationships and its effect on the life of the body.

Eventually, Chekhov left Tolstoy behind as he charted his own unique path in Russian literature. A physiologist, he did not tolerate romanticized or unrealistic treatments of the body. Even as he praised Tolstoy's art in his 1889 story about a man's jealous murder of his wife, "The Kreutzer Sonata," he excoriated him in an 1890 letter to Pleshcheev for the boldness with which he expounds upon matters that he does not understand and that out of obstinacy he does not want to understand. So, his views about syphilis, foundling homes, women's disgust for sexual intercourse, and so on, not only can be challenged, but in fact, betray an ignorant man who has not attempted during his long life to read two or three books written by specialists.

Tolstoy was always deadly serious in his treatment of moral issues. Chekhov responded as a scientist, humanist, and doctor who never strayed from the basic realities of the human body. After an initial period of strong and direct Tolstoyan influence, irony began to infiltrate the dialogue when Chekhov addressed sexual themes, as in the 1894 story, "Anna on the Neck," a mirco-parody of *Anna Karenina*. And in 1894 he wrote to Suvorin:

Tolstoy's philosophy affected me strongly, held me in its

spell for 6 or 7 years; what attracted me were not the basic tenets, which I already knew, but Tolstoy's manner of expressing himself, his way of thinking, and possibly a kind of hypnotism. But now something in me protests; reason and justice tell me that there is more love for humanity in electricity and steam than in chastity and abstention from meat.

Unlike Tolstoy, with his panoramic visions and the great moral dramas that infuse every detail of his works, Chekhov's ambitions centered on the unique individualism and integrity of each living creature; his stories are anchored in his characters' perceptions of the world, which join with those of other characters, even though they see differently. Whereas for a writer like Dostoevsky the material world is, as Chudakov put it, "the first step of a staircase leading upwards," Chekhov's heroes "cannot tear themselves away from the earth."

The theater

The late 1880s saw Chekhov's first major theatrical success. Drama was part of his life from beginning to end—from amateur theatricals and sneaking into the theater in Taganrog to the triumphant premiere of The Cherry Orchard on the Moscow Art Theater stage in 1904. A complex mix of factors contributed to his playwrighting: personal taste, social contacts, financial incentives, and his utterly unique artistic sensibility. Chekhov was a social being, and he spent a lot of time with "theater people." Drama begins, but does not end, with the text of the play. The tangibly collaborative and social aspect of the art was to Chekhov's taste. He enjoyed attending rehearsals and consulting with a production's actors and directors, and many of his close friends were theater professionals. In some spheres acting was considered a disreputable activity for women; his story

"The Chorus Girl" offers what feels like an authentic picture of the marginal life of those in the lower realms of the profession. In his stories and plays provincial actresses have a hard life, and success is hard to come by. Chekhov always appreciated actresses as human beings, as colleagues, and as artists in their own right. Many of the women he was close to were actresses, including Lily Markova, Kleopatra Karatygina, Lidia Yavorskaya, and Ludmila Ozerova, with whom he had affairs of various lengths and degrees of seriousness; he met Olga Knipper, also an actress, in 1898 and married her in 1901. Even in his narratives, Chekhov never stopped thinking like a playwright. His drama and his stories treat the same themes and feature understatement, mood, and interactions among characters, rather than heroism and dramatic action. Some stories are constructed according to dramatic principles: chapters that progress from one discrete scene to the next; carefully crafted dialogue and staging; a plot climax that occurs in the story's equivalent to Act III. There is a kind of higher-level symbiosis for Chekhov between the two genres. For that reason, when reading Chekhov's plays, it may pay off to consider them to be stories that lack a narrator; likewise, when reading his stories, it can be a good exercise to separate out the narrator's discourse from the interactions and conversations among characters and the course of the plot. Compare Dostoevsky, who never published a play, but whose famous novels can be read as melodramas plus narration, featuring careful scene construction, suspense, and dramatic pacing, particularly in the so-called "scandal" scenes, where all characters are brought together for passionate argument, slaps on the face, tossing of 100,000 rubles into the fire, fainting, sudden revelations, and the like. What was innovative about Chekhov's work in both his stories and his plays, was their anti-dramatic nature and their focus on the stuff of ordinary life.

For Chekhov money was always a factor in his writing, determining to some degree how much to write, and in what genre. Plays were a reliable source of income, particularly given that each performance would bring in additional royalties. In 1887-8 he wrote one-act plays, The Bear, The Proposal, and Swan Song, which are still performed on stage around the world and are an enduring staple in acting school curricula and dramatic competitions. In 1887, he wrote a long play, Ivanov, at the request of Feodor Korsh, who ran a successful private theater in Moscow. The advantage of Korsh's theater was that plays in a private theater were not subject to the burdensome administrative procedures and censorship of the state theaters. The premiere of this, Chekhov's first full-length play to reach the stage, set a pattern for his future plays: even as it defied conventions and expectations, it provoked strong audience reactions. Korsh's audiences expected comedies–and Chekhov conceived the first version of Ivanov as a comedy, but its adulterous protagonist suffers depression throughout the play, shuns and betrays his Jewish wife, and dies at the end–in the first version, of a sudden heart attack and in the later Petersburg version, of suicide. The audience alternatively hissed and applauded. Two years later, Suvorin and Chekhov undertook to produce each other's plays: in 1889, Chekhov supervised the production of Suvorin's Tatyana Repina, in Moscow, and Suvorin produced Ivanov in St. Petersburg. The play brought in several hundred rubles–considerably more than he earned from his stories. Its success, artistic and monetary, spurred Chekhov's work on his next full-length play, The Wood Demon, during his second summer at Sumy. The Theatrical-Literary Committee of the state Alexandrinsky Theater in St. Petersburg had several objections to the play: it was critical of a university professor, was more novelistic than dramatic, and lacked a strong plot. So Chekhov turned it over to a Moscow theater, the Abramova group, which had broken away from Korsh. The premiere in November 1889 was widely panned as a mismatch between content and genre, and Chekhov withdrew the play. At some point over the course of the next seven years, he rewrote The Wood Demon into the masterpiece Uncle Vanya.

By 1890, Chekhov was a famous story-writer and playwright. He was well-established in the publishing world, with influential colleagues and strong friendships. His financial stresses had eased.

His family had moved into stable lodgings. But the intensity with which he had addressed the big existential and ethical questions in his latest works showed deeper tensions at work. In 1890, a complex mix of professional, emotional, and personal forces combined to send him on a radical new step in his life's journey: a grueling overland trip across Siberia to the prison colony on the island of Sakhalin off Russia's far eastern coast.

5. Sakhalin

The distance between Moscow and Vladivostok on the Far East coast of Russia is 5621 miles by rail. In the 21st century—2019, to be precise—a traveler wishing to cross Siberia from Moscow to Vladivostok in 13 days could purchase an "Imperial" class ticket for a VIP suite on the Trans-Siberian railway's Golden Eagle for $17,417.90. The suites, on offer from the "Luxury Train Club," have "individually controlled air conditioning, a private bathroom en suite: shower, wash basin, toilet"; passengers are provided with bathrobe and slippers, and travel "in splendor amidst opulent décor." They are invited to view the passing countryside through panoramic windows, "whilst enjoying delicious cuisine." In 2019, if you were in a hurry to cross these eight time zones, you could luck into a $330 plane ticket that would get you to Vladivostok in eight and a half hours (nonstop). Sakhalin Island is another 740 miles to the east; a flight takes just under four hours at a cost (in 2019) of $128.

In Chekhov's day, however, there were no airplanes or automobiles, and though European Russia was well connected with rail lines, the trans-Siberian railroad did not yet exist; the link between Moscow and Vladivostok was completed in 1904, the year of Chekhov's death. There were not even any reliable roads for wheeled traffic through the vast expanse of Siberia. At first glance, a map does not suggest insurmountable geographical barriers beyond the Ural Mountains, which run north to south, dividing European Russia from Asian Siberia. But the obstacles are considerable. Traveling over snow in a fast sleigh drawn by the famous Russian three-horse troika can be efficient and even romantic, with its cozy bear rugs and sleigh bells, but more than a few hours of it can get cold, and if your runner breaks off, or something happens to the horses, frostbite can kill you in a matter of minutes. Temperatures in Siberia career wildly, depending on the season—from as low as 60 degrees Fahrenheit below zero in the winter to as high as 100 in the summer. The monstrous mosquitoes that swarm Siberia by the millions in the summer are legendary; they can drain a caribou calf within minutes, and though they do not carry disease, they can drive their human victims crazy with itching and pain. In the spring the snows melt and rivers overflow their banks, inundating the land for miles around. The west-east traveler faces the annoying fact that Siberian rivers run north-south, so the only way to manage boat travel is by taking massive zig-zags, and switching often from wheeled to keeled vehicles. It made a lot more sense for a 19th-century voyager just to get on a boat in Odessa on the Black Sea and go by sea around the south of Asia, bypassing the entire continent.

The real question is why anyone would make this trip to begin with. Explorers, prospectors, religious dissenters, military personnel, and government officials had their reasons. Siberia is the world's largest continuous land mass, contiguous with the "stans" of Central Asia and with China, and as such bears momentous political importance. Its mineral wealth is legendary, and for centuries questers have thronged East in hopes of making their fortune–this is not all that different in spirit from the American settlers' push into the western wilderness through the 19th century. An underappreciated factor in the Siberian migrations has been Russia's strenuous efforts to colonize–mostly successfully–this vast land. The Old Believers who split off from the Russian Orthodox church in the 17th century established settlements in Siberia; pockets of them can still be found there today. Many of the travelers to Siberia had been involuntary–notably, convicts serving time in Siberian prisons or living there in exile. Guarding them, too, was not anyone's first choice for a career. The most famous 19th-century Siberian prisoners were convicted of political crimes: the Decembrists–elite young noblemen who had staged an ambitious uprising in St. Petersburg in 1825; Polish revolutionaries; Dostoevsky and other members of the Petrashevsky group in 1849; radical writer Nikolai Chernyshevsky and various terrorists beginning in the 1860s, and many more, including Vladimir Lenin, who spent from 1897 to 1900 in Siberian exile. Though Siberian prisons are best known for their role in Stalin's Great Terror—the waves of political arrests, executions, and sentences to exile and incarceration in the state prison system (the GULAG), beginning in the 1930s—the majority of prisoners, then as well as in Chekhov's time, were criminal convicts: murderers, rapists, thieves, kidnappers, counterfeiters, embezzlers, and the like. Chekhov's Siberian odyssey in the spring and summer of 1890 was a complete anomaly. He was a private individual, not a gold prospector, government official, convict, explorer, religious dissenter, or political activist. Contemporaries in the literary world were baffled—though liberals were impressed, likely because of the trip's potentially political nuances. Was it flight or quest, or some mixture of the two?

Chekhov's motivations for his Sakhalin trip were many, and ultimately not as mysterious as they have sometimes been made out to be. Personal, professional, psychological, familial, and romantic factors all played a role. A yen for travel may have been built into his character, both on the quest side and on the flight side. Alexander Chudakov suggested that Chekhov was drawn to "other worlds," both in space (to Algeria, to the far North), and in time ("200-300 years from now"); when loquacious dreamers like *The Three Sisters'* Vershinin begin to philosophize, they dream of what life will be like in a time that is far, far away—as far as Sakhalin is from European Russia, or even farther. Chekhov took many journeys in his lifetime, some unexpected, some brief, some for his health, and one—this one—epic. His attraction to travel resonated obliquely with his careful protection of his privacy. He was meticulous and conscientious in meeting his obligations to family, publishers, and friends, and he spent a lot of time in the company of others, but he fully protected the sanctity of his inner life. He was notoriously reluctant to commit to the many women with whom he had relationships. So successful was he at this, that nearly a hundred years after his death he had the reputation of an ascetic when it came to women. A desire to be alone certainly played a role in his Sakhalin decision. And as a writer, it was natural for him to seek new impressions through travel.

The yen for travel

Deeply encumbered in relationships with family and friends, not to mention professional commitments, Chekhov had a tendency to flee emotionally fraught situations. In 1887, exhausted and overworked as a writer, doctor, and family member beset by sick relatives, he bolted suddenly for the Crimea. In the summer of 1889, all the Chekhov siblings gathered in Sumy, where Nikolai was dying. But on June 15, within an hour after his brother Alexander's arrival to Nikolai's bedside, Chekhov—recall, he was a doctor with a particular skill in diagnosis, and knew full well his brother's dire medical condition—abruptly departed with a couple of companions for Poltava, 100 miles away. When Nikolai died two days later, Anton had to turn around and take the long journey back, changing trains and enduring involuntary waits in gloomy stations along the way. In 1889, without explanation, he traveled to Crimea instead of going on a planned trip to Western Europe with Suvorin and Grigorovich, where his mail was being sent, and where Grigorovich went to meet him at the train station every day. After the stormy premieres of his plays—Ivanov and, especially, The Seagull—Chekhov fled. Ivanov premiered in Moscow on November 19, 1887; he left soon after for St. Petersburg; After The Seagull's first performance in St. Petersburg on October 17, 1896, he disappeared that very night and left for Melikhovo, without saying goodbye to his hosts or the many people involved in the production. The yen for the road never abated. The Russian biographer Alevtina Kuzicheva tracked Chekhov's travel, arguing that it was fear of death that prompted him to journey to places far and near. Indeed, while terminally ill in the spring of 1904, Chekhov came up with the completely insane idea of traveling to the Far East to serve his country as a military doctor during the Russo-Japanese war. And shortly before his death that summer, while a complete invalid in Badenweiler, Germany, Chekhov was making plans to travel to northern Africa—a bizarre fantasy that is perhaps the only, and oblique at that, explanation for the enigmatic map of Africa hanging on the wall in Uncle Vanya.

Though highly sociable, Chekhov craved solitude. And he had a deep respect for travelers, adventurers, and explorers—people who did the opposite of sitting at desks and writing made-up stories. In 1888, he wrote an obituary for the famous Russian explorer of Siberia, Nikolai Przhevalsky, who had died alone on an expedition to Central Asia. Chekhov praised his heroism, contrasting it to the work of city-bound intellectuals. The lone traveler, venturing bravely into unexplored territory untouched by modern civilization, had a strong appeal for the writer jaded by the intricacies of literary politics, the demands of his profession, and the pressures of his many relationships. At the end of the 1880s, the "wild East" may have been more appealing to him than the trip to Western Europe that his literary mentors had been urging him to take with them. What Chekhov needed at that point in his life was not more civilization and more "literature," but less. Sheer curiosity, a desire for new impressions, for a completely unfamiliar environment, clearly played a role in his decision to head east. Ultimately, Chekhov's journey to Sakhalin represents the purest form of freedom, a primeval declaration of independence from everything that constricted him materially, politically, intellectually, and socially. The great irony is that he sought this freedom in a prison colony.

The trip to Sakhalin promised respite from the wearying routines and relationships complicating his life in Moscow. These relationships, as always, included romantic entanglements. In 1889, his sister Masha had brought home a friend who was teaching with her at a girls' school in Moscow—an extraordinary 19-year-old beauty, Lika Mizinova. She and Chekhov were strongly attracted to each other, and their relationship was to continue for several years—though with notable interruptions along the way, including liaisons with other women. It is likely that an affair he had with an actress, Kleopatra Karatygina, which began during his trip to Crimea in 1889, played a role, if minor, in his decision to go to Sakhalin. Karatygina was considerably older (by 12 years) than Chekhov, and would never have been a serious candidate for a life partner, and in fact, he insisted on keeping their relationship secret. But she was from Siberia, and as he began planning his trip, she was able to give him a great deal of information and practical advice. From January to March 1890, Chekhov delegated his sister and his female friends—Lika and Olga Kundasova ("the astronomer")—to help him with research for the trip. It might have even been his sure knowledge that they would soon be parted that enabled his intimacy with Lika to grow.

By 1890, Chekhov's long-term responsibilities as head of the household—now primarily consisting of his parents and sister Masha—were beginning to ease. He could be confident that they could survive without him for a few months, and in any case, he would continue to ensure their financial welfare from a distance. His brothers lived independently, and he himself had not yet married or started a family. The timing was fortuitous. Chekhov was maximally free.

Justice, humanity, and science

As for political motivations, the 1880s were marked by strict censorship and surveillance of literary figures—including Chekhov, though he had not betrayed any inclination for political activism; he was busy studying, doctoring, writing, and providing for his family. His works, though their humor was often satirical and occasionally skirted the edges of dissent, generally avoided politically sensitive themes. Chekhov was, in his own way, a patriot, and as is clear to the reader of *Sakhalin Island*, he supported—though never stridently—Russia's colonizing mission in Siberia. His friendship with Suvorin and publication of his works in *New Time* alienated the liberals of his time. In turn, the often primitive or superficial nature of political dialogue among his contemporaries alienated him, and he fervently professed his freedom from any agenda. But political reform is only one aspect of much deeper ethical and philosophical issues, and there is no doubt that during this time, as throughout the 1890s, Chekhov was preoccupied with questions of freedom and justice.

Though Suvorin's side of the correspondence has been lost, from Chekhov's extant letters to him it was clear that the Sakhalin trip was the subject of intense conversations, and, given Suvorin's extremely conservative political views, undoubtedly arguments, between them. On March 9, 1890, Chekhov wrote Suvorin a detailed rationale for his journey:

> You write that Sakhalin is of no use or interest to anyone. Do you really think that? Sakhalin could be of no use or interest only to a society that doesn't send thousands of people into exile there, spending millions to do so. With the exception of Australia in the past, and Cayenne, Sakhalin is the only place where one can study the use of convicts for colonization. [...] Sakhalin is a place of unbearable suffering, the worst suffering of which man, whether free or subjugated, is capable. [...] it is clear that we have allowed *millions* of people to rot in prisons, to no purpose, without thinking, barbarously; we have driven people through the cold, in fetters, tens of thousands of versts [Russian units of distance equal to 0.6629 mile], have infected them with syphilis, have corrupted them, have multiplied the numbers of criminals, and have blamed it all on red-nosed prison wardens.

Questions of basic humanity and justice were clearly on Chekhov's mind, as was his sense of responsibility to contribute meaningfully to society and to alleviate injustice by any means within his power. The American scholar Robert Louis Jackson found a quiet and even Biblical power in Chekhov's language in letters related to the Sakhalin trip, reminiscent of the Old Testament story of Exodus. The prisoners, quite literally as well as deeply figuratively, were the exiled and homeless people of God. Upon his return from Sakhalin in December 1890, Chekhov wrote Suvorin again: "God's world is good; the only thing is not good: ourselves." And Siberia became, in a trope that Dostoevsky had made familiar in his *Notes from the Dead House*, a vision of hell. Other scholars, such as Michael Finke, have emphasized these tonalities, identifying Chekhov's trip as a katabatic journey–that is, to hell and back.

With a few exceptions, such as his letters to Suvorin, momentous questions of justice and freedom remained latent in Chekhov's communications about his expedition–before, during, and after. His primary explicit motivation for the trip to Sakhalin was to conduct demographic research. He had always craved the opportunity to focus on serious scholarly work and clearly wanted to engage in socially useful activity. He had not yet abandoned his "wife"–medicine (science). And indeed, the months he spent on Sakhalin were fully devoted to his research–not in a dusty archive, but in thousands of encounters with living human beings.

An arduous journey

Chekhov spent the winter of 1889-90 preparing for the trip. With the help of family and friends, he researched Siberia and Sakhalin, assembled paperwork from the authorities in St. Petersburg, packed, and made financial arrangements. The journey began on April 21 with his departure from Moscow for Yaroslavl. From there, he set off down the Volga river, and then the Kama, to Perm, where he boarded the train for Ekaterinburg and beyond. At Tiumen, he switched to horse-cart for the arduous journey overland to Irkutsk near Lake Baikal, where the road ended. This leg of his journey, through which Chekhov–suffering his usual aches and pains relating to tuberculosis, digestive issues, and hemorrhoids–endured unimaginable hazards from snow, flooding, freezing rain, rotten food, potholes, drunken traveling companions, a cart accident than nearly killed him, and many more unpleasant adventures–took two months. Though in a letter to his family on May 20 he wrote that he was in good health, on the same day he reported to Suvorin that, "from the lack of sleep, the constant trouble with my baggage, from the bouncing around and hunger, I suffered a hemorrhage that ruined my mood, which was already pretty bad."

The experience of traveling alone through the vast inhospitable environment of central Siberia brought on a moment of existential crisis, a confrontation with death that, according to the critic Radislav Lapushin, Chekhov experienced on the banks of the cold and flooded Irtysh River. He recorded the episode in a May 7 letter to Maria Kiselyova: "And here I am sitting at night in a hut that stands in the lake on the very shore of the Irtysh, I feel a clammy dampness through my whole body, and a loneliness in my soul, I listen to my Irtysh beating against coffins, to the wind roaring, and I ask myself 'Where am I? Why am I here?'" Chekhov later gave the hero of one of his Siberia stories, 'In Exile,' these very same thoughts.

The payoff for his suffering was the stunning landscapes, especially in the Baikal region. Chekhov wrote his family on June 6: "The feelings that I had when I saw the mountains and the Yenesei compensated me a hundredfold for all the trouble I had been through, and forced me to curse Levitan for his stupidity in not coming along." After a stressful wait for a steamer's arrival—an event highly unpredictable in those parts—he crossed the lake. Baikal, the deepest body of fresh water in the world, is a mile deep; its stunning beauty sent chills down Chekhov's spine, and again made him curse Levitan, one of Russia's greatest landscape painters, for not being there to put this extraordinary scenery on canvas.

From Baikal Chekhov rushed east on hired horses in relays to Sretensk on the Shilka River, from which point on the trip became easier, as he could travel by river steamer.

East of Baikal, the Chinese elements are everywhere. Russia and its politics fade into the background, and, paradoxically, in this land that is basically one great prison, freedom fills the air. Chekhov wrote his family on June 23-26 from a steamer that has run aground on the Shilka in a remote place called Ust-Strelka: "The air on the ship gets red hot from the conversations. Here people are not afraid to speak loudly. There's no one here to arrest you, and nowhere to exile you to, so you can be as liberal as you want."

There's plenty of time to kill when you're stuck in the middle of Siberia. In that same letter, Chekhov reported a conversation in which he asked a fellow "grounded" passenger when he thought they would be able to proceed along their way. The man countered, "Don't you like it here?" Indeed, Chekhov thought, "why shouldn't we stay, so long as it's not boring?" Here again, we must pause for contemplation—just as Chekhov did on that boat. Turns out, Siberia, the world's most notorious place of imprisonment, is a place of maximal freedom. Perhaps this was, most of all, what Chekhov was seeking.

Between his arrival on Sakhalin on July 11, 1890, and departure by sea from Vladivostok on October 19, Chekhov traversed the entire island, conducting personal interviews with convicts and exiles in every settlement on Sakhalin. The work was meticulous and exhausting, and he did not stop until he was done. On a total of 10,000 separate census cards, accounting for every involuntary resident on the island, he noted down each individual's name, address, marital status, age, religion, birthplace, year of arrival, literacy level, source of income, and medical history. Chekhov disarmed his subjects, among whom were some of Russia's most vicious and terrifying criminals, spending the rest of their lives in shackles, or even chained to wheelbarrows. There's no evidence he was ever in danger from any of the people he encountered there—a testament to his extraordinary combination of empathy, restraint, self-effacement, and acute qualities as a listener. All of this goes to explain Chekhov's famous "humanity"—a word by which his contemporaries and readers characterized him.

Sakhalin Island

Among the factors that sent Chekhov to Sakhalin, any purely literary motive seems minimal–the trip could more plausibly be attributed to a desire to flee fiction writing than to seek out new material. He did write, though it was something completely new and different. There was a key writerly precedent. In 1859, Dostoevsky had returned to St. Petersburg after nine years in Siberian prison and exile. In 1861-62 (Chekhov's baby and toddler years), he published *Notes from the Dead House*, a memoir of his experiences in the hard-labor camp, thinly disguised as a novel. The book became an instant best-seller for its sensational, detailed account of a sphere completely unfamiliar to law-abiding European Russians; it serves to this day as the primary point of origin and model for Russia's very rich tradition of the Siberian literature of prison and exile. Though Chekhov's literary sensibility was antithetical to Dostoevsky's in almost every way, and though his recorded references to him were few, it would have been natural to expect him to contribute to this tradition. Remarkably little fiction emerged from Chekhov's Sakhalin observations and experiences. The writings related to his trip took four forms: (1) his ethnographic, demographic, statistical study *Sakhalin Island*; (2) travel notes (*From Siberia*); (3) letters; and (4) a handful of short stories: ("Gusev," 1890), "Peasant Women" (1891), "In Exile" (1892), and "A Murder" (1895), plus scattered elements in other works.

Sakhalin Island, the longest discrete work in Chekhov's oeuvre, is a monumental opus that equals Dostoevsky's *Notes from the Dead House* in scope, despite the differences between the two works. Dostoevsky's book takes the form of a first-person observation of the human types and interactions among inmates in a hard-labor prison, structured around a highly symbolic trope of death and resurrection. Chekhov's is a work of journalism and research, fully empirical and quantitative in nature, written in his inimitably precise and engaging style. In *Sakhalin Island*, the author conveyed the distinguishing qualities of the individuals he encountered and of their grim environment, fraught with disease, prostitution, ignorance, despair, and violence. The book's focus is ruthlessly external and empirical, and the reader feels the force of Chekhov's restraint, his conscious effort to renounce any trace of the subjectivity and interiority of artistic fiction. With deep regret, we also feel the weight of countless Sakhalin stories that he did not tell, and that would never be told. Chekhov began writing the book upon his return to Moscow at the end of 1890 and published it in several issues of the thick journal *Russian Thought* in 1893 and 1894. The book represents a remarkable achievement. Truly ahead of its time, *Sakhalin Island* is an early "big data" project, one that is a valuable source for historians, geographers, demographers, and ethnographers to this day. To his contemporaries, though, as with any pioneering work, his project of conducting a census of the entire population of the island was bewildering.

The book shows two sides of the observational sensibility that was at work, though in different proportions, in Chekhov's fictional writing as well. He zoomed in and panned back. Even as he conveyed a sense of the uniqueness and integral value of each individual human being, he strove to generalize, learn, measure, and gauge a truth based on meticulous observation and quantitative aggregation of data. The Sakhalin trip gave Chekhov the opportunity to fully actualize the "objective" and empirical side of his intellect, setting to one side the necessary imaginative element that is so central to his—and any—fiction. Chekhov never created "types." His characters never serve exclusively to illustrate an idea, philosophy, political stance, or message. They show their individuality with every feature, every thought, utterance, and action; this is what makes Chekhov's characters feel so real to readers—despite the basic fact that he made them up. The "real people" on Sakhalin, too, come alive as individuals even though they served as data points. But his overriding purpose was scientific—to create a complete and objective description of the population of involuntary residents on the island. In doing so, above all, he treated each one of them with the respect that they probably had never experienced before, or would ever again.

It was primarily Suvorin's funding that enabled Chekhov to make his trip. He published his travel notes, *From Siberia*, in Suvorin's *New Time* in June, July, and August issues that summer. His third "writerly" product from the trip was the letters he wrote to his family and friends from Siberia. These are among the most expressive and eloquent letters in his whole oeuvre; their quality reflects the striking novelty of what he encountered and observed; it also reflects the fact that he did not write any fiction during the journey—pouring all of his creative power instead into these writings.

It is interesting, though given Chekhov's goals and the nature of his experiences during the summer of 1890 not surprising, that his Sakhalin trip left so little tangible trace on his fiction. But the one story he wrote based on his experiences of the sea journey home, "Gusev," is extraordinary in its power. A rapt or rash reader might even suggest that this story alone justified the whole journey. "Gusev" recounts the deaths of two steerage-class passengers who die of illness on a ship in the South China Sea. One is a Russian peasant-class common soldier with a mythical world view and an unquestioning Christian faith and acceptance of his fate; the other is a radical intellectual who calls himself "protest incarnate." Both die and are cast into the sea. We have been inside Gusev's mind; he died at some point, though we did not notice exactly when. In the end, we—whoever we are—see him from outside. We watch as Gusev's body slowly descends down, passing through a school of fish, who themselves observe, enthralled, as below them a shark lazily opens his great jaw with its two rows of teeth and tears from end to end the sailcloth that Gusev is wrapped in. Then we too are gone, and the great sky opens out:

> Meanwhile, overhead where the sun sets, clouds are gathering; one cloud looks like a triumphal arch, another like a lion, a third like scissors ... From behind the clouds a broad

green ray appears and reaches to the very middle of the sky; a little later a violet-colored one lies next to it, and next to it a gold one, and then a pink one ... The sky turns a tender lilac color. Looking at this grand, enchanting sky, the ocean first frowns, but soon itself takes on colors that are caressing, joyful, passionate, colors that human language finds it hard to name.

That meditation on death that Chekhov experienced on the banks of the Irtysh River, he had at last transformed into immortal art.

After passing through the Suez Canal, Chekhov finally arrived in Odessa in early December, went through a brief quarantine, and boarded the train for Moscow, arriving home seven and a half months after he had left. Travelers to Sakhalin can visit two Chekhov museums there—one in Yuzhno-Sakhalinsk commemorating the *Sakhalin Island* book, and the other, a "house museum" in Alexandrovsk.

6. Melikhovo

Chekhov loved animals, except cats. When he returned from Sakhalin to Moscow in December 1890, he brought two small animals that he had purchased in Colombo, Ceylon, now Sri Lanka. At the time he thought they were mongooses, but one of them turned out to be something meaner–an untamable palm civet. Chekhov described the creatures as "a mixture of rat and crocodile, tiger and monkey." Often commented on by visitors, the mongooses played a prominent role in the Chekhov family's life for the next year and a half, complete with bolts for freedom, near-death experiences, and attacks on unsuspecting family guests, until ultimately one–the palm civet–seemed to have perished in vague circumstances and the other was dispatched to the Moscow Zoo. Later, in 1893, Chekhov acquired two pureblood dachshunds, Bromide Isaevich and Quinine Markovna, from one of his editors, Nikolai Leikin. The two dogs were members of the family, and Anton used to conduct hilarious long conversations with them, entertaining guests and family. His brother Mikhail recalled in his memoirs:

> Every evening Quinine would go up to Anton Pavlovich, place her front paws on his lap and gaze adoringly into his eyes. He would change his facial expression and in a broken, old man's voice would say, "Quinine Markovna!... You poor thing! You should go to the hospital! ... They'll fix you up!" He'd talk for a half hour with the dog, and everyone in the house would die laughing. Then it would be Bromide's turn. He would also put his paws on Anton Pavlovich's lap and the show would start up again. "Bromide Isaevich!" Chekhov would address him in a voice full of concern. "How can it be? The archimandrite got stomach cramps, and he went behind the bushes, and the boys snuck up and sprayed him with

water from the hose!... How could you let that happen?" And Bromide would growl angrily.

When he returned to Moscow from his trip, Anton was exhausted; he fell ill and spent his first weeks at home recuperating. In January 1891, he went for three weeks to St. Petersburg, where he stayed with Suvorin and socialized with colleagues and friends in the city. His social circle included a number of female friends who had waited eagerly for his return, including Lika Mizinova and other old friends like Olga Kundasova (the "astronomer"), and newer ones, including various alluring St. Petersburg actresses. There were many demands on his time; Sakhalin and its needs were fresh on Chekhov's mind, and he made the rounds soliciting contributions for charitable enterprises on the island, notably orphanages for street children and child prostitutes. He also arranged for shipments of thousands of books and supplies to schools on the island, and began writing *Sakhalin Island*.

In March, Chekhov took his first trip to Western Europe, together with Suvorin and Suvorin's son, Alexei Jr., a.k.a. "the Dauphin." They visited Vienna, Venice, Rome, Naples, Nice, and Paris before returning home in mid-May. In Pompeii, an ample dose of fine red wine one day over lunch prompted Chekhov to venture up Mt. Vesuvius. The horseback ride to the foot of the mountain, as he wrote his family on April 7, left him with a feeling that he'd been summoned into the secret police office and thrashed. After an arduous, nearly four-hour climb, he contemplated the crater from the rim:

> The soil all around, covered with a layer of sulfur, sends up clouds of vapor. Stinking white smoke, sparks, and molten stones belch up out of the crater, and under the smoke lies Satan, snoring. A cacophony of sound: waves crashing on the shore, thunder from the heavens, the clattering of rails, beams falling to the ground. It's terrifying, but at the same time, you feel like leaping down into the very maw of the volcano. I now believe in hell.

Unlike many of his Russian literary predecessors and contemporaries, Chekhov had not become fully fluent in any foreign language, though he would master French later in life. He said once: "I know all languages except foreign ones." And unlike famous Russian intellectuals who had emigrated westward–political radicals like Alexander Herzen and liberal Westernizers like the novelist Ivan Turgenev, he was not drawn to Western Europe as a place of residence. Though duly impressed with European art, architecture, history, and appreciative of the freedom of expression he found there, he showed no regret upon returning home. Some discomfort on this particular trip was occasioned by financial considerations; the Suvorins were extraordinarily wealthy, sparing no expense on their accommodations abroad. Anton wrote home that the family would have no money for the whole summer: "The thought of it ruins my appetite. For a trip that I could have done solo for 300 rubles, I've borrowed a thousand. All our hopes rest on the fools who will put on amateur productions of my *Bear*." Though Suvorin was one of Chekhov's very closest friends, he was also an employer who paid him for his writing and published many of his stories. Suvorin was accustomed to living at a level of luxury completely alien to Chekhov's experience. When Chekhov visited the Suvorins in St. Petersburg, he was given luxurious accommodations, elaborate meals, and his own valet. He often felt in Suvorin's debt, and monetary imbalance was a constant throughout their years of friendship. It did not help that despite Suvorin's generosity and goodwill, the accounts of *New Time* were often chaotic, such that payments to Chekhov were frequently delayed or imprecise.

New home in Melikhovo

The Chekhovs had moved out of their lodgings on Sadovo-Kudrynskaya (the "red cupboard"), which had become too large for them in Anton's absence, as the family scattered and the flow of guests subsided. In the summer of 1891, Anton rented a dacha at a large estate in Bogimovo, some 110 miles southwest of Moscow, which later served as the prototype of the artist's home in "The House with the Mezzanine" (analyzed in Chapter 3). Here he worked intensely on two projects, *Sakhalin Island* and the long story *The Duel*, set on the Black Sea coast of the Caucasus and featuring an extended argument between a Darwinian scientist and a classic Russian "superfluous man" type. As for Lika Mizinova, she had chosen to spend the summer not with Chekhov but at the home of a relative, not coincidentally near where Levitan was staying with his mistress, the married dilettante artist Sofia Kuvshinnikova. When Lika–undoubtedly fed up with Chekhov's inability to commit to her despite their mutual attraction–ignored his jocular letters inviting her to come visit, and Levitan himself wrote, teasing Chekhov about his own fondness for her, Chekhov sat down and dashed off his notorious "The Grasshopper" (analyzed in Chapter 3), featuring the guilty parties in starring roles. The story precipitated a scandal among the literati, and more importantly, a painful break with Levitan.

Meanwhile, the family was searching for a house with land where they could live permanently. Though Chekhov had originally hoped to move to the Ukrainian countryside, a suitable property of 600 acres, Melikhovo, turned up 45 miles south of Moscow. Travelers would ride the Moscow-Kursk rail line to Lopasnya station, then slog, slide, or bump six miles through mud or snow along a primitive, rutted road to the house. Though now Chekhov was earning a decent income from his writing, he had to take on a 10-year mortgage to buy the property, and to borrow 5000 rubles from Suvorin for the down payment. The Chekhovs moved to their new home in early March 1892. While the prospect of homesteading was attractive in the abstract, they soon encountered a mass of unexpected woes: the house was dark and small, infested with bugs, and in dire need of repair; the river, pond, and woods on the property turned out to be grander in name than in reality; the water supply was primitive, and plumbing nonexistent. The farm machinery and implements were profoundly inadequate to their tasks; the animals were scant and in poor health, and the fish in the pond died en masse. Workers were drunk or otherwise unreliable. Far from relieving financial pressures, the purchase of the estate intensified them. Within a few years, in November of 1896, part of the house was destroyed by fire. Having witnessed fires in the area, Chekhov had taken care to insure his property and acquire a "fire machine" that could pump water from the pond next to the house, but this calamity entailed yet another round of construction and hassles with materials and paperwork.

With the purchase of Melikhovo, the Chekhovs' years of living in rented urban lodgings ended, and years of manual toil, gardening, and farm management began. The core residents were Pavel Yegorovich and Evgeniya Yakovlevna, Masha, and Anton, though Masha taught in Moscow on weekdays, and Anton traveled frequently. They drew upon the local population for household help and farm labor. Family and friends came and went, including Ivan, a schoolteacher, and the youngest brother Misha (Mikhail), in between jobs in the tax service. Misha described life at Melikhovo vividly in his memoir of Anton. In addition to making necessary improvements in the house, the family raised livestock, cleared the land for an orchard and garden, enlarged the pond near the house, and stocked it with fish. In "Gooseberries," from the 1898 Melikhovo cycle The Little Trilogy, Chekhov told the story of a city man who toils away writing documents in a government job. He dreams of moving to the countryside and living in the lap of nature as he had in childhood, when he had frolicked in the woods and fields, fished, and admired the flora and fauna. Most of all, he craves the taste of home-grown gooseberries. After years of self-denial, scrimping, and saving, he finally manages to buy an estate. His brother, the story's narrator, comes to visit and describes the newly minted landowner as bloated, lazy, and gone to seed, the property unimpressive, and the long dreamed-for gooseberries sour. The host, though, is in ecstasy when his first crop of gooseberries is served. He gobbles them down greedily, exclaiming at how delicious they are. The guest sees only the ugly side of the landowner's life; the host—only the joys. Both viewpoints may represent the author's own experience: the owner (a former paper-pusher, which, at least in externals, likens him to the author) takes pride in his property, even as it drains the life from him.

When Chekhov moved in, word spread immediately that the new neighbor was a doctor, and patients began to line up outside his door. He treated the locals, mostly for little or no pay, throughout his time in Melikhovo. He also became very active in public service. There were enough troubles to go around. Poor weather in 1891-2, compounded by logistical, political, and economic factors, had brought on a famine throughout central Russia. Conditions were compounded by a cholera epidemic, which threatened to reach Melikhovo. Chekhov had gotten involved in famine relief efforts beginning in the fall of 1891. Public service was never easy in imperial Russia; government officials were mistrustful of private initiatives, which smacked of liberalism and made their own work seem ineffectual. Embezzlement of funds was common. In the winter of 1891-2, Chekhov joined an ingenious scheme initiated by a friend, a local council official Yevgraf Yegorov. To prevent starving peasants from selling their horses so they could afford to feed themselves, the scheme gathered funds to purchase the horses, keep them fed over the winter, and then sell them back to the peasants on credit in time for spring planting. By July 1892, Chekhov was also working tirelessly with the regional Public Health Board in its anti-cholera efforts—work that probably helped prevent the disease's spread in the area. Though Chekhov spent the whole summer fund-raising, examining and treating patients, gathering information, working to improve sanitary conditions, and participating in meetings with local and district officials, he turned down the financial stipend he was offered for this work. This would be a pattern throughout these years; for Chekhov, service was service, not work to be compensated financially. In January and February of 1897, he helped conduct the census of the local population, a trivial undertaking in comparison with his monumental Sakhalin feat, but arduous nonetheless. In January 1897, he wrote Suvorin: "The census-takers have been given disgusting inkpots, disgusting badges like brewery brands, and briefcases that the forms don't fit into, so the impression is of a sabre that won't slide into its sheath. Shame! Starting in the morning I go from hut to hut, knocking my head on low door frames that I'm not used to, and my head throbs hellishly; I have migraine and influenza." During his travels around Melikhovo in connection with these activities, Chekhov encountered the full range of human misery and corruption, and would incorporate his observations into powerful works like "Peasants," *Uncle Vanya*, and "In the Ravine." We will take a close look at key Melikhovo works, loosely observing chronology, but taking some loops backward and forward to address key themes.

Works inspired by Melikhovo experiences

Chekhov's experiences with famine relief provided him with material for the 1892 story "The Wife," which treats the theme of charity through the lens of an unhappy marriage. Other works of the Melikhovo period dramatize the problem of "great" versus "small" deeds. The artist protagonist of "The House with the Mezzanine" remains passive, faced with the enormity of the social problems plaguing humanity; meanwhile, his antagonist, the young landowner Lida, works tirelessly to improve conditions among the local peasants. In Russia, the conflict was momentous; acting locally to tackle social ills—as Chekhov did in Melikhovo—could, according to critics of the system, perpetuate deeper, systemic patterns of injustice. Meanwhile, dreaming of large-scale systemic change had contributed to Russia's historical patterns of radicalism and revolution. In "Ward no. 6," Chekhov's protagonist cites Stoic philosophy to justify his passivity, exemplifying Chekhov's lifelong preoccupation with the ethics of thinking versus acting. For the writer, the "thinking" part poured into the characters' words, and into the meticulous poetic construction of the text. In his own daily life, though, Chekhov had no patience for idealists, and threw himself into action when there were problems to be solved. His commitment to local action reflected his mission as a healer, his focus on the absolute integrity of each individual, and his mistrust of all abstraction. The Chekhovian answer to the accursed question, "what is to be done?" was not to talk, but to act. As, in his own life, he did.

Schooling had been the key to raising Chekhov up out of the lower classes, and he demonstrated a lifelong commitment to education in his writing, personal acts of charity, and public service. At various times in his life, he provided supplies and funding to individual students in need, and during the years he lived in Melikhovo, he took an active interest in the state of schools in the district. Rural teachers faced almost impossible obstacles: schoolhouses were decrepit; supplies, from books to firewood, were scarce; students' families were disrespectful; school officials were corrupt and cynical; and teachers' salaries were at a starvation level. Ultimately, with much effort, Chekhov built three schools in the area. This, like his other public-service activities, entailed fundraising among the local nobility as well as from sources in the city, taking valuable time away from doctoring and writing. In one masterpiece, My Life (1896), Chekhov's vivid description of the difficulties the idealistic protagonists face as they build a local school draws upon autobiographical experience.

Chekhov's writing about the heroism of teachers reflects a deeper dynamic at work: the human struggle for civilization against the inertial forces of nature. There is something particularly Russian about this struggle; great novelists like Nikolai Gogol (Dead Souls, 1842) and Ivan Goncharov (Oblomov, 1859) had produced epic descriptions of the clash between an "active hero" and a natural environment dominated–along with its inhabitants–by organic processes of decay. Gravity pulls the human individual ever downward to inevitable decline and death. On a larger scale, the same forces threaten not just Russian institutions of education, literature, government, and economy, but all of world civilization. Educators are front-line fighters on this battlefield. They do for the human mind and memory what gardeners do for the land. Though in some works Chekhov satirized teachers ("The Man in the Case," 1898) and mocked the pretensions of pedants (*The Wood Demon; Uncle Vanya; The Three Sisters*), he described the lot of the rural schoolteacher in an 1897 story, "In the Cart," with extraordinary sympathy and understanding:

> It's cold in the morning; there's no one to heat up the stove; the guard has gone off somewhere; the students start to arrive at the crack of dawn, tracking in snow and mud; they are noisy; everything is so awkward and uncomfortable. The apartment is just one room, including the kitchen. Every day after school her head hurts; there's a burning in her chest after dinner. She has to collect money from the children for firewood and for the guard, and turn it over to the school guardian, and then entreat him, this smug, rude peasant, to send firewood, for God's sake. At night she dreams of exams, peasants, snowdrifts. And this life had aged her, had made her rough and unattractive, angular, clumsy.

Chekhov always avoided abstraction. In this story, he demonstrated that heroism is a matter of daily labor, patience, and integrity. The teacher, Marya Vasilievna, persists in doing her duty day after day, unrewarded, undistracted by illusion:

> Teachers, low-wage doctors, medical assistants, overwhelmed with work, cannot even comfort themselves with the thought that they are serving an idea, or the people, since their heads are constantly full of thoughts about a piece of bread, about firewood, bad roads, illnesses. It's a hard, tedious life, and the only people who can endure it for any length of time are silent workhorses like this Marya

Vasilievna; as for those active, nervous, impressionable people who talk about their calling, about service to an ideal, they soon wear down and gave up the cause.

Marya Vasilievna had taken the job out of necessity after her parents died. Her memories of her previous comfortable life fade from her mind under pressure of her daily struggles. For her, teaching is just a job, there is nothing fancy about it. But by removing all abstraction from her work, Chekhov showed its true heroism. Even as she struggles to remember her own mother's face and her happy childhood, Marya Vasilievna serves as repository and guardian of all human knowledge, a front-line fighter to preserve memory, knowledge, and civilization against the forces of ignorance, inertia, and decay.

This same struggle dominated Chekhov's life in Melikhovo, where he poured energy into cultivating his land. When looking for a property, Chekhov had sought an estate with a garden on a river, and one of his criteria was that it be well-kept; the neglected and overgrown gardens of romantic literature held no appeal to him, beyond as a setting for doomed trysts. At Melikhovo, Chekhov and Masha created a lush garden and orchard, and Pavel Yegorovich tended it diligently. They researched horticulture, and sowed and tended an abundance of vegetables and flowers, including exotic varieties. In Russian the word, *sad*, can refer to both a garden and an orchard; gardens and orchards served as the setting of works of all periods and genres, from the short 1880 story "Because of Little Apples" to the last play, *The Cherry Orchard*. The Melikhovo garden and orchard resonate deeply in Chekhov's writing of this period. The setting operates on many levels: material realism, reflecting the writer's daily experience and observation; political and social themes (the collapse of the Russian landowning class); ethical and cultural issues (the struggle between positive action and organic decay); and mythological and religious allegories. Chekhov's literary gardens drew on the Genesis story of the fall from Eden—the human plunge from innocence into knowledge and sin. All of these themes come together in "The Black Monk" (1893), a vivid and terrifying depiction of mental illness, told from inside the mind of the sufferer. The story's protagonist, Andrei Vasilyich Kovrin, a scholar at the university, suffers a breakdown from overwork–which in his case means too much thinking and writing. To convalesce, he goes to the country to stay with former neighbors, a landowner Yegor Pesotsky and his daughter Tanya, who have been like family to him since childhood. Through years of hard work, the father has cultivated a fine orchard which, over and above its beauty, brings substantial profit. Tanya, tells Kovrin, her guest, childhood friend, and future husband: "Everything here is just the garden, the garden, the garden and nothing more. [...] Our entire life, all of it, has gone into the garden; all I dream about is apple and pear trees." The orchard–let us call it all of world civilization–thrives only at the cost of tireless, constant labor, performed under the ruthless management of Tanya's father–a stern patriarch out of the Book of Genesis. Kovrin, Tanya, and farmhands stay up all night tending fires, whose smoke prevents frost from damaging the trees. The image of the thick, caustic, black smoke spreading across the earth under the trees recurs later, vertically, in the form of a vision of the titular black monk, who appears only to Kovrin and tells him he is a genius, different from ordinary mortals. When Kovrin, inevitably, marries Tanya, her role changes from sister figure to wife. With marriage comes the fall, and underlying it all, Kovrin's growing insanity (which he perceives as a higher knowledge, accessible only to great thinkers like himself), marked by conversations with the monk. Over and above its Biblical nuances and the multilayered setting of the garden, "The Black Monk" headlines Chekhov's depictions of mental illness–shown from inside–and as such is a classic of world literature. Kovrin's bloody death from a lung hemorrhage at the story's end draws upon Chekhov's medical knowledge as well as his awareness of his own illness and impending death.

Chekhov focused on medicine, mental illness, and passivity in the face of social problems in another important Melikhovo story, "Ward No. 6," published in the summer of 1892. Its protagonist,

Dr. Andrei Yefimych Ragin, is responsible for a squalid, locked psychiatric ward, housed in a filthy outbuilding on the territory of a provincial hospital. The untended, overgrown grounds of the hospital yard convey the consequences of Ragin's failure to tend his garden. The doctor spends his time reading quietly at home, ignoring the patients in his care. He justifies his idleness with quotations from the stoic philosophy of Marcus Aurelius:

> And why prevent people from dying, if death is the normal and proper end of each individual? What difference does it make if some merchant or government worker lives an extra five or ten years? If the goal of medicine is to be seen in the ability of medication to relieve suffering, then the question arises: why relieve it? First of all, they say that suffering leads man to perfection; and, secondly, if humanity actually figures out how to relieve its suffering with pills and drops, then it will give up religion and philosophy, in which up to now it has found not only protection from all kinds of misfortunes, but also even happiness.

On a rare visit to the ward, Dr. Ragin is drawn into conversation with one of the patients, Ivan Dmitrych, a young man suffering persecution mania. They argue ethics. When the doctor attempts to convince his (neglected) patient that all happiness lies within, Ivan Dmitrych counters:

> A teaching that preaches indifference to wealth and the comforts of life, and contempt for suffering and death, is completely incomprehensible for the vast majority, since this majority has never known wealth, or the comforts of life; to have contempt for suffering would mean for them to have contempt for life itself, since man's entire being consists of sensations of hunger, cold, injury, loss, and a Hamletian fear of death.

Even as he went to the heart of this philosophical debate,

Chekhov–here and everywhere–embedded words and ideas in a fully realized world of stage, character, plot, and action. His careful construction of this world conveys the devastating human consequences of the doctor's, and anyone's, passivity. Dr. Ragin intellectualizes in the comfort of his clean, subsidized apartment, fed by his housekeeper on a regular schedule, and surrounded with books. Meanwhile, in the ward for which he is responsible, Ivan Dmitrych suffers filth, hunger, and involuntary confinement, not to mention the brutality of the thuggish peasant guard Nikita. Nikita is the most "active" character in the story, not a talker or a thinker–to put it mildly; as such, he occupies the opposite extreme of the thought-talk-action moral spectrum from the doctor, and demonstrates the consequences of his philosophy. Ultimately and inevitably, the doctor himself is locked into the ward, where Nikita beats him viciously, and he dies. The story's structure features a classic balance between points of view and a plot trajectory leading to a climactic moment of dramatic irony: the doctor becomes patient and tastes the barren fruit of his philosophy.

"Ward No. 6" is justifiably among Chekhov's most famous works; here, more powerfully than anywhere else, he demonstrated the ethical implications of an adherence to any abstract philosophy when there are things to be done. The story can be read on many levels. It offers an exposé of political and social conditions in Russia during Chekhov's lifetime; allegorizes the country as one great prison; explores the human condition and the problem of freedom; and examines the ethical costs of stoicism. Though "Ward No. 6" is not recognizably autobiographical in its surface details, the story conveys the author's most profound introspection on the "big questions," informed by his years of medical practice, his long-standing interest in mental illness, his experience with corrupt officialdom during the famine and cholera efforts, his quiet preoccupation with injustice, and his tangible encounter with the human costs of incarceration on Sakhalin. Reading "Ward no. 6," we are reminded that Chekhov is the only great Russian writer whose experience of prison was voluntary. This story is the fruit of that odyssey.

The problem of anti-Semitism disturbed Chekhov throughout his life. In "Rothschild's Violin" (1894) he tackled the issue head-on, presenting it as one melody line woven into a multilayered symphonic matrix. Like other Chekhov masterpieces, it can be read as an improvisation on a theme—in this case, that of a wooden box. The coffin-maker Bronze, a Christian Russian, earns money by playing violin in a Jewish orchestra. Not enough people are dying in his village, so to comfort himself for his "terrible losses,"—the lack of income—"he would place the violin next to him on the bed at night; when he was troubled by thoughts, he would touch the strings, and the violin would make a sound in the darkness, and he would feel better." A violin is shaped like a woman, we infer, and Bronze sleeps with the wooden box—which takes the place, it seems, of his long-suffering, abused, and neglected wife. Meanwhile, she falls ill, and even as she lies on her sickbed, he measures her for a coffin. Soon afterward, she dies, after briefly mentioning a little daughter who had died some 50 years earlier. Bereaved, guilty, and now suffering his own terrible loss, Bronze goes down to the river where he sees a lone weeping willow tree, itself with a large cavity in the trunk. "How it [or "she"] had aged, the poor thing!" he thinks. Suddenly he has a vision of the child that he and his wife might or might not have had—he can't remember. Decades before, the last time he'd been down to the river, a lush birch forest had stood on the opposite bank; the river and its banks had been rich with fish and game, and boats had sailed along it, bearing abundant cargo. Now it was all bare except one tree, "young and supple, like a nobleman's daughter." Where have all the trees gone? Gone to wooden boxes, every one: coffins, the violin, boats, Bronze's workshop—itself a wooden hut clothing the man. The boxes are cases—for the body, itself a shell for the soul; the coffin itself is the ghost of a cradle that was not made. Was there a child, or was she always just a tree, weeping? The coffin, the violin, the wood, all of it proceeds along the violin-shaped Mobius strip that loops between the present, bereaved reality, and the lush past, or dream reality—with its joy, its love, a child, a soul. When his own death comes upon him, Bronze bequeaths the violin—not a coffin, not something to be sold or a box for a body to lie in—to Rothschild, a musician in the local Jewish orchestra whom he, along with the entire village, had mocked and abused throughout his life. The music of Chekhov's story acts on the reader like the music from that violin—bearing the soul of the bereaved, the suffering, the sorrowful, and the deceased characters in the story, and the rest of us out here in life.

Other famous prose works written in Melikhovo include "A Woman's Kingdom" (1894), about a young woman who has inherited a factory she does not understand how to manage, and "The Student" (1894), a short story—which at one point Chekhov claimed to be his favorite—about a divinity student who, on his way home for Easter, tells the story of the disciple Peter's renunciation of Jesus to two peasant women he encounters. Set in a merchant milieu in Moscow, *Three Years* (1895), one of his longest works, treats married life not as the fulfillment of idealistic or romantic love, but in all its human complexity as it changes through time. "Ariadne" (1895) reflects, cruelly, elements of Lika Mizinova's sad story that year. The previous winter Lika had begun an affair with one of Chekhov's friends, the writer Ignaty Potapenko. They traveled to Paris, where even as her lover set up a household with his second wife, Lika languished in a hotel room, pregnant with his child. Abandoned and alone, far from friends and family, Lika sent pleading letters to Anton. Even though he traveled to western Europe with Suvorin again in the fall of 1894, Chekhov did not visit her. Lika gave birth to a daughter, Christina, in Paris in November of 1894, and ultimately brought her home to be raised by her family. Meanwhile, Chekhov occupied himself with other women, including Lidia Yavorskaya, an actress, and Tatyana Shchepkina-Kupernik, a writer, themselves a couple with some notoriety in the theater world.

The Seagull and "Peasants"

In 1895, Anton retreated into a small guest house the family had built on the Melikhovo grounds: "I'm writing a play. [...] I'm writing it not without pleasure, though am committing terrible violence to the conventions of the stage." This work was to be *The Seagull*, the first of Chekhov's four major plays, and it would usher in a new era in world theater. The play reflects details from Chekhov's own experience as a doctor and writer, and, like many works, can be read as an allegory of the artistic process—complete with a muse, fishing metaphors, and two writers: one representing hard work, the other, creative inspiration, and both—aspects of Chekhov himself. It incorporates multiple elements from the lives of Chekhov's closest friends: Lika's ill-fated affair with Potapenko and the birth of her child, as well as episodes from Levitan's life and the lives of the Suvorins. The play even sends a coded message to Lidia Avilova, one of many women who deluded themselves into thinking Chekhov loved them, and other micro shout-outs to acquaintances. In the spring of 1892, just before the publication of "The Grasshopper," which precipitated Chekhov's three-year break with Levitan, the writer and the artist had gone hunting at Melikhovo. Levitan shot and wounded a snipe; at his request, Anton killed the bird to put it out of its misery—an incident reflected in the play. In 1895, after the two had reconciled, Levitan attempted suicide after a rash affair with the daughter of his lover at the time. Unlike at other key moments when loved ones needed his care, Chekhov dropped everything and rushed to his friend's side. Back in 1887, Suvorin's 21-year-old son Valerian, a budding playwright, had shot himself. Konstantin Treplyov, the younger writer in *The Seagull*, bears elements of the frustrated, innovative artist reminiscent of Suvorin's son and of Levitan. The play builds quite consciously on the deceased father-mother-son drama of Shakespeare's *Hamlet*, and at the same time incorporates elements from the avant-garde theater that was seeping into Russia from France during those years. And the titular symbol recalls Ibsen's play, *The Wild Duck*. The weight of all these elements is borne by an artistic structure that introduced something completely new to the Russian stage—small talk and trivia dominating the onstage time, with tragedy lurking unnoticed offstage. The greatest tragedy was yet to come. In art, as in life, Chekhov's diagnostic sense was downright terrifying. In the play, the heroine Nina, who runs away from her young admirer Treplyov with the older writer, Boris Trigorin, gives birth out of wedlock to a baby who dies. Eerily, within a month after the play's premiere, Lika's two-year-old daughter, Christina, became ill and died.

The Seagull's debut was—and remains to this day—one of the most famous episodes in the history of world theater. After last-minute edits to satisfy the censor (Potapenko, despite serving as the prototype for Trigorin, managed the process on Chekhov's behalf), and after inadequate rehearsals, it premiered at St. Petersburg's Alexandrinsky Theater on October 17, 1896. *The Seagull* was the right play in the wrong city, the wrong theater, the wrong director, the wrong staging, the wrong actors, and the wrong audience. Tone-deaf critics, jealous of Chekhov's talent, packed the hall, waiting and eager for failure. Also present in the audience were the very friends whose personal tragedies were to be exposed onstage—Lika and Potapenko foremost among them. All of these factors led to predictable results: an epic scandal in the hall. Chekhov fled immediately to Melikhovo to lick his wounds. In his absence, and despite the disastrous first night, the play's subsequent performances were successful, and perceptive members of the audience realized that they had witnessed something extraordinary.

Meanwhile, Chekhov vowed never to write for the theater again—fortunately, a vow he did not keep—and occupied himself with something completely different. Russian writers had long been preoccupied with the problems faced by Russia's peasantry. The 1861 emancipation had given new freedoms to a vast population that lacked the economic means to take advantage of these newfound opportunities, not to mention education and proper health care. Idealistic young liberals had sought to help the peasants by going out into the country and, among other things, teaching them to read and write. Writers like Dostoevsky and Tolstoy had offered their own airbrushed visions of the peasant in famous works like "Peasant Marei," Notes *from the Dead House*, and *Anna Karenina*. Chekhov's contribution to this conversation was, like all his contributions to discussion of the big Russian questions, short and devastating.

In March 1894, responding to Tolstoy's idealized views, Chekhov had written to Suvorin: "Peasant blood flows in my veins, and you cannot impress me with peasant virtues. From childhood, I have believed in progress, and I cannot help but believe in it, since there is a huge difference between the time when I was thrashed and the time when they stopped thrashing me." In "Peasants" (1897), the characters live short, brutal lives dominated by misery, filth, violence, drunkenness, and ignorance. Like other Chekhov stories, "Peasants" can be read as an exposé of conditions of life of a particular Russian milieu, as a composition on the theme of judgment, or as an allegory for the human condition. A former peasant, who has been working in Moscow as a waiter, falls ill and goes home to his village to recuperate, taking with him his wife and little daughter, Sasha. There they stay with his family—parents, sisters-in-law, a drunken brother, and children, including a little girl Motka, who live in crowded, squalid conditions in a one-room hut. Motka is wild, uneducated, and dark-skinned from the sun; Sasha is a fragile, pale little angel from the city (a.k.a. from another world) who reads aloud from the Bible. Both girls violate their granny's commandment to watch the geese and are flogged—introducing the theme of guilt that will quietly dominate this profound story. Late one night, while the peasant men drink in the village tavern, a hut catches fire. The vivid description of the fire at the story's climactic moment reflects Chekhov's own observations and experience in Melikhovo; at the same time, coming on the heels of the girls' sin, it can be read as a depiction of the Last Judgment, complete with doves flying across the sky, a black stallion running loose, and the wailings and flailings of sinners on the charred ground. As such, the peasant village that serves as the setting of this story can be seen as a microcosm of the world as a whole—we are all sinful peasants, who get an occasional glimpse of a world beyond. In the end, little Sasha—newly fatherless—and her mother Olga—newly widowed—wander homeless from village to village. Within a year, their author would be compelled to leave his home too, when illness forced him to depart from Melikhovo.

This happened at the end of March 1897, when Chekhov was in Moscow to read proofs of the "Peasants" manuscript, which he sent to *Russian Thought* on March 17. While there, during dinner with Suvorin, he suffered a massive hemorrhage and was taken to the eminent Dr. Ostroumov's clinic to be diagnosed and treated. From then on, he could no longer deny his tuberculosis. Among his visitors was Tolstoy, with whom Chekhov discussed immortality, a conversation that was soon followed by a second hemorrhage. Just the previous month, Chekhov had copied into his diary from his notebook his most famous statement about religion: "Between 'there is a God' and 'there is no God' lies an enormous field, which the true sage crosses only with great difficulty. But a Russian knows only one of the two extremes—the middle between them does not interest him." Though Chekhov's literary territory was, in fact, this vast middle field, he occasionally, and memorably, depicted the extremes as well: in "Gusev" and "The Black Monk," the Genesis story of the Creation and Fall and, in "Peasants," the Apocalypse.

Though the elder Chekhovs continued to live in Melikhovo for another couple of years, this moment essentially ended the Melikhovo period of Chekhov's life; doctors ordered him to move to a warmer climate, which, in this age before antibiotics, was the only treatment for the disease. In Chekhov's case, this meant spending winters in Nice, in the south of France, and, ultimately, in Yalta on the Crimean Black Sea coast.

Reflecting the writer's deeply held values of cultivating the earth through gardening, and cultivating human minds through education, the house and garden at Melikhovo have been lovingly restored as a museum and very active cultural center. The Melikhovo House Museum is the world's major center for scholars, ordinary readers, schoolchildren, theater lovers, and students interested in Chekhov's life and works.

7. Yalta and Western Europe

After spending a quiet summer convalescing in Melikhovo, Chekhov headed to France in the fall of 1897. He settled in Nice, where he took up residence at the "La Pension Russe." Though ill, he was able to resume writing, producing fine stories like "In the Cart," "The Pecheneg," "At Home," and "A Visit to Friends." The Russian cemetery and white church, high on a hill above the city, and the feelings of homesickness that he experienced there, left their mark on the profound late story "The Bishop." While in Nice, Chekhov developed friendships with members of the Russian expatriate community, visited nearby casinos, followed the Russian as well as the French news, and worked to improve his French. Though generally restrained in expressing political views, he took a stand in favor of Alfred Dreyfus, the Jewish officer who had been sentenced to life imprisonment on a trumped-up charge of espionage. The anti-Semitic stance of the editors at *New Time* damaged Chekhov's relationship with Suvorin, who had been one of his closest friends and confidants for 10 years.

Upon his return to Melikhovo in May of 1898, Chekhov wrote stories that would be among his most famous, including *The Little Trilogy*. Two friends have gone out hunting in the Russian countryside; in the evenings, each one tells a story: "The Man in the Case" and "Gooseberries." They visit a local landowner, who tells the third story, "About Love." Though each tale seems to offer an obvious moral—for example, about freedom, or the need to avoid complacency or to be true to oneself—the deeper meaning lies in the narrative frame and context, in the way the story is told and heard. In "Gooseberries," for example, the narrator, contemplating his brother's contentment with his house and land, lies awake, fuming about people's smugness in the face of all the world's injustice: "Outside the door of every satisfied, happy man, someone should be standing with a little hammer, knocking continually to remind him that no matter how happy he might be now, sooner or later life will show him its claws; misfortune—illness, poverty, loss—will befall him, and no one will see or hear him, just as now he does not see and hear others." It's hard to disagree that the world is full of injustice, and that people should work to make things better. But the narrator's words betray a deep dissatisfaction and misery that is his alone, and the reader would do well to ask why his brother's (or any other person's) personal happiness should be so upsetting to him. In "About Love," the narrator tells of years of love for a married woman that failed because both parties were afraid to admit their love. Even through our tears, attentive readers may deduce, based on the story's depiction of the external signs of the woman's happy marriage, that the narrator was deluding himself the whole time, and that the whole affair had taken place completely in his mind. In that case, "About Love" might be interpreted as a sort of meta-story about how stories are created, or about the myths we tell to comfort ourselves. "The Man in the Case" tells of a provincial schoolteacher, Belikov, who tormented his colleagues and students by a pedantic adherence to rules and regulations. But given that after his death nothing changes in the town, the reader must ask why everyone blames him. All three stories, read together, represent the finest manipulation of the storyteller's art. In all of Chekhov's works, the reader must always be alert to who is telling the story, and be suspicious of anything that may seem to be a clear moral. More often than not, the joke is on the narrator, or, let us own this, on us.

As I have been suggesting throughout this book, Chekhov's master trope is the image of the material case, or shell. Readers of fiction tend to focus on character and plot—*who* does *what*. But Chekhov's stories and plays are profoundly spatial in their sensibility. *Where* things happen is equally important. Chekhov's "where" clings to the human being in the form of a shell, like a snail's, that serves as both clothing and home, sheltering the vulnerable, squishy soul cowering inside. The shells that concern Chekhov are man-made cases; through time and the plot's progression, life proceeds from case to case—cradle to coffin—with a series of cases in between. The trope is concentric: body, home, town, country, world. The boundary between character and setting in Chekhov's works, as we have seen, can be porous. At key moments, the cases that surround, shelter, and confine his characters open out to the natural world. In The Steppe, Yegorushka's departure from home and family leaves him maximally vulnerable, "unshelled." As he travels through the steppe, he merges with nature, and with the consciousness of everyone else—other travelers, flora and fauna, the reader, and the author. Trapped in his case, Belikov does not experience this form of liberation. He surrounds himself with protective armor, cowering in his jammies and canopy bed at night, and enfolding himself in layer after layer of clothing, hat, umbrella, and the lid of his carriage, during the day. The school's routines and the rules he clings to are just another manifestation of his case. Where does Belikov end and his environment begin? The "shellishness" that Chekhov seems to mock in this profound story is in fact something all human beings share, a terror of the unknown, a fundamental underlying principle in the writer's epistemological poetics. This fear takes a variety of pathological forms, from agoraphobia to consumerism and hoarding, as people strive to reinforce the material buffers between themselves and the unknown. The trope underlies Chekhov's master plot of homelessness in the plays Uncle Vanya, The Three Sisters, and The Cherry Orchard, which all tell of families on the brink of losing their homes.

This point at which the material case ends is Chekhov's focus despite his professed materialism. We move outward through our shells—body, clothes, room, house, city, country, world—and from there into that raw, mysterious unknown beyond the last outer layer of the sky, which we contemplate, for example, at the end of "Gusev." Or we move inward: from the cosmos and all of that, through my room and my clothes, my body, but then what? And this soul thing deep inside, how is it different, or even separate, from that soul thing out there beyond the last shell that we can see? Mysteriously, they are the same. When Belikov dies at the end of his story, his case opens out, and his secret inner life—infused with suspicion, pettiness, and paranoia—spills out into the world, a world which, after his death, does not change, though he is dead and tucked snugly in his perfect coffin case. The message parallels, though with a radically different tonality, the ending of "Rothschild's Violin," when Bronze dies and his suffering melts away, leaving only the wooden case and a beautiful, sad song that fills the world.

Chekhov's busy final years

A letter awaited Chekhov upon his return to Melikhovo from Nice in May 1898. Vladimir Nemirovich-Danchenko, a playwright, acting teacher, and director, had written to ask permission to put on *The Seagull* with a new company he was forming, together with Konstantin Stanislavsky, a wealthy actor and director. The Moscow Arts Theater (MAT) aimed to move beyond the star-centered, melodramatic conventions of the day, and to develop productions that staged the whole text as a work of art, drawing upon the contributions of each actor working in ensemble. Though leery after this play's disastrous premiere in 1896, Chekhov finally agreed to give it to MAT, and in September, he attended the first rehearsal. Before leaving for Yalta, where his illness would keep him through the winter, he also attended the company's rehearsal of another play, and was impressed by the performance of one of the actresses, Olga Knipper, who was also to play the role of Arkadina, the aging actress in *The Seagull*.

Under the shadow of his illness, Chekhov needed to establish a more suitable place of residence and to get his affairs in order. In mid-September 1898, he fled the unhealthy Moscow climate for Yalta in the Crimea. There he found two properties to buy, a small Tatar farmstead high above the coast west of Yalta, and another, a lot at Autka, above town, where he decided to build a house. His parents were still at Melikhovo, where his father worked from dawn to dusk taking care of the farm. Within a month of his arrival in Yalta, though, Anton received the news that Pavel Yegorovich had died suddenly of an abdominal rupture after straining himself. With Chekhov no longer able to live on the estate and his father gone, Melikhovo was an empty shell. He held onto it for the time being, as he settled into Yalta and began writing again: "An Incident at Practice," "The New Dacha," "On Official Business," and "The Darling" (or "Angel"). In this last story, a woman takes on the personality of the men she loves. Tolstoy read it with delight, seeing the heroine as an ideal of self-sacrificing love. Readers who value feminine agency, though, or who detect a destructive force at work in the premature deaths of the beloved men, have been horrified by the story for over a hundred years.

In Moscow, *The Seagull* opened on December 17, as much a triumph as its original St. Petersburg premiere had been a disaster. The production reflected MAT's respect for the play's text as an integral work of art, brought to life by the company's actors and director working together. Chekhov's last four dramatic masterpieces—the latter two yet to be written—were instrumental in the development of this collaborative artistic milieu, and ultimately were key to the theater's artistic and financial success. His growing attachment to the actress who played Arkadina, Olga Knipper, was closely intertwined with his relationship with MAT. Olga was a professional actress, devoted to her art, which meant that she had to stay in Moscow through the winter months—precisely the time Chekhov could not live in or near the city. He fully supported her career, so even as their love developed, the two were separated for months at a time, even after their marriage in May of 1901. This separation sparked some 800 eloquent and moving letters between the two.

In early 1899, after long negotiations through an earnest but not too effective intermediary, Chekhov sold the rights to all his works for 75,000 rubles to Adolf Marx, a shrewd publisher who ran the journal *The Cornfield*. The contract provided Chekhov with a large sum of cash, to come in three installments of 25,000 rubles, guaranteeing his financial independence and that of his heirs–essentially his sister Masha and his mother–for the rest of his life and theirs. His friends were aghast at the terms, though, which seriously undersold his intellectual property. The contract required that Chekhov collect and provide final versions of his works, including early stories that had been signed with pseudonyms and scattered in various publications years before. Chekhov decided not to include a number of early pieces–as many as 200–but he spent considerable effort revising and refining the ones he selected. Though friends and colleagues, mindful of his health, rallied and helped locate and retrieve these works, preparing the manuscripts took valuable time away from creative work. This was and remains an incalculable but not total loss; the revisions he made to early works made them into true masterpieces. Readers can get a sense of these changes in the Russian academy edition of Chekhov's collected works (1973-83), which provides detailed information about the writing process for each story, as well as complete listings of his edits.

In Yalta, Chekhov spent time with major writers of his era–Maxim Gorky, the future "proletarian" writer who later headed the Soviet Writers Union; Ivan Bunin, who emigrated after the Bolshevik Revolution and in 1933 was the first Russian to win the Nobel Prize for Literature; Alexander Kuprin, a prose writer popular at the time; and Tolstoy, who came to Yalta in 1901 to recuperate from a serious illness. Bunin and Gorky both wrote famous reminiscences about Chekhov's life during this time. Though Tolstoy loved both Chekhov and many of his stories, he claimed that his plays were "worse than Shakespeare's" and felt "The Peasants" to be an outrage against the Russian peasant. Chekhov continued to be socially active in Yalta; he contributed to efforts easing the lot of many impoverished people, ill, like Chekhov, with tuberculosis, who came to the city to convalesce or die. He also served on the board of the Yalta Girls' High School, and was involved in the Red Cross and in famine relief. During the latter years of his life, he was also a generous mentor, and took time to read the manuscripts of beginning writers and give them advice. Many of these writers have been long forgotten, leaving only gaps in Chekhov's creative legacy, which, as elsewhere and at other times, were filled with service to others.

In August 1899, Chekhov sold Melikhovo. Like his other financial dealings during this period, the terms were disadvantageous, but there was no reason to keep the estate, and no one to live there and manage the property. After the sale, he returned to Yalta, where he could move into his half-completed house, the "white dacha." After the success of *The Seagull*, MAT had asked for *Uncle Vanya*, which had been staged quietly in the provinces. Chekhov had written the play at some point during the 1890s, drawing on material from his earlier play *The Wood Demon*. Though originally the play was considered for production in a state-sponsored theater in St. Petersburg, the censors' disapproval of its irreverent portrayal of the pretentious Professor Serebryakov freed it for staging in a private theater. MAT premiered *Uncle Vanya* in October 1899 in Moscow, with Olga Knipper playing the seductive beauty Elena—Serebryakov's second wife—and Stanislavsky in the role of Dr. Astrov. The play is often cited for its environmental message; the doctor—who bears autobiographical traits—advocates for the preservation of Russia's forests. Like all of Chekhov's works, though, its primary value lies in its musicality, balance, and psychological insight, as well as its hints at allegory. The Voinitskys—Vanya (Ivan—John—everyman) and his sister Vera ("Faith") are members of the declining landowning nobility. Vera, Serebryakov's first wife, had married "down," for he was of a lower social class. After Vera's death, her brother Vanya and daughter Sonya ("holy wisdom") toil together on the country estate year after year, sending all the money to her father—who has become an eminent professor—and his new wife Elena in the city. The young stepmother who had studied piano before her marriage is the Russian equivalent of Helen of Troy and represents pure beauty and art; her name also bears the Russian root for "idleness" (*len'*). When Elena and her husband come out to the country to visit, her beauty infects everyone around her with idleness, particularly the hardworking Dr. Astrov—in whose hands rest not only the health of the people who live in that area, but also the preservation of the natural environment. With Elena around, no one can focus on work. Typically for Chekhov, love is not distributed equitably. The careful reader will realize that all the tensions in the plot lead back to the death of Vanya's sister, a memory so terrible we never learn what happened. And though viewers will sympathize with the victims, there is enough responsibility to go around. We cannot survive without work, but what value is there to a life devoid of beauty?

"In the Ravine" and "The Lady with the Dog"

Despite Chekhov's illness and all the efforts he spent on finances, editing, living arrangements, and paperwork, in 1899 he produced two masterpieces: "In the Ravine" and "The Lady with the Dog." The magnificent "In the Ravine" chronicles the fall of a prominent, but corrupt and degenerate family in a rural Russian town against the background of the country's growing industrialization. The beautiful and hardworking but viperlike daughter-in-law Aksinya, though promiscuously unfaithful to her clueless, deaf husband, is barren. The other daughter-in-law, also beautiful and hardworking, but painfully naïve and still in her teens, has been brought in to marry the other son, Anisim. Though he is utterly indifferent to her and leaves days after the wedding, somehow, over the course of their short conjugal encounter, the two of them manage to conceive an heir. Before long, Anisim is arrested for counterfeiting, dispossessed, and sent to Siberia with a man who may or may not be his lover, but most certainly is his accomplice and the mastermind of his crime. Jealous Aksinya, enraged that her naïve sister-in-law's child will inherit the family's property, murders the baby by scalding him with boiling water. With its stark opposition between innocence and guilt, the story improvises on the word "sin," in Russian "*grekh*." The patriarch's wife clucks when she talks, like a mother hen, "*Okh tekh tekh*," and the sounds mingle with the rattlesnake-like clicking of the keys that homicidal Aksinya carries around while doing household chores, and with the ominous jingling of counterfeit coins being thrown down the well, marking the triumph of sin over innocence. And though the crime was committed in broad daylight, the murderess gets away with it. All the witnesses—basically everyone in the story—are complicit, deaf, powerless, or passive. Radical critics and readers praised the story as an attack on capitalism, though its true value is as high tragedy, a Russian *King Lear*.

"The Lady with the Dog" offers that rarest of rarities, a Chekhovian story of requited love. In its details, the story reflects Chekhov's own romance with Olga. By depicting an adulterous affair involving a heroine named Anna, but without a hint of judgment or disapproval, Chekhov offered his answer to Tolstoy's great tragic novel, *Anna Karenina*. The story features a theatrical construction, with distinct scene changes that reflect the changing of the seasons and the development of love, even as the characters continue to live their mundane family lives: Yalta—Moscow—the provinces—Moscow. The heroine, a provincial official's wife, enters the scene quietly (with her famous little white dog), mingling with other vacationers on the Yalta embankment. There is nothing special about her, and she blends in with the crowd. She catches the eye of an experienced seducer, Dmitri Gurov, who expects nothing more than a casual fling, and undoubtedly has gone to Yalta for precisely that purpose. They go their separate ways after a brief affair, but mysteriously to them both, their love fills their lives, until it is the only thing that gives them meaning, though nothing changes externally. Only occasionally do they manage to get together, keeping their trysts completely secret. "Anna Sergeevna and he loved each other like intimate family members, like husband and wife, like tender friends; it seemed to them that fate itself had predestined them for each other, and it was incomprehensible how they could be married to different people; they were like two migratory birds, male and female, who had been caught and forced to live in separate cages."

The extraordinary power of this story draws on its depiction of the secret core of love, that, though trapped in the cage, or, shall we say, the *case*, of every physical barrier, stage setting, and social convention that surround human beings, makes life worth living. This inner mystery, as in all of Chekhov's best works, opens out to the universe in the famous Oreanda scene, where, as Anna and Gurov sit looking at the sea, they merge with something greater than themselves. In this story Chekhov, whose works abound in instances of failed communication, finally allowed characters to understand each other completely—beyond the banal words they speak. The predictably judgmental criticism from contemporary conservative and tone-deaf readers ("an apologia for immorality..."; "a sacrificial offering to animal lust...") can be interpreted as yet another manifestation of the cage within which Anna and Gurov, miraculously, savor and nurture their love.

The Three Sisters and other late works

In April 1900, the Moscow Arts Theater brought its repertoire, including *The Seagull* and *Uncle Vanya*, on tour to the Crimea. Chekhov joined them in Sevastopol, saw their productions, and hosted them in Yalta. After they went back to Moscow, Chekhov took a short trip there himself to spend time with friends and with Olga, before returning to Yalta. Ultimately, the couple were able to spend several weeks together that summer—leaving a tantalizing gap in the otherwise regular flow of letters. During this time, Anton began work on his next play for MAT. *The Three Sisters* chronicles the decline of a landowning family, whose refinement, erudition, and appreciation of the finer things in life render them vulnerable to crude but powerful forces from below. The brother, overeducated, coddled, and passive, marries a woman whom the sisters disdain for her lower-class origins and lack of refinement. The sister-in-law, Natasha, possesses alarming fertility, and each new baby pushes the sisters inexorably from their home like some primeval, organic force of nature. The play, like other Chekhov works featuring the landowning gentry, reflects greater trends in Russian society during this time, the end of an entire way of life. MAT desperately needed this play (and the next one, *The Cherry Orchard*), as it worked to build its artistic tone, identity, and reputation, not to mention ensuring a firm financial foundation. Chekhov continued working on the play after Olga returned to Moscow in August. From the city, she wrote a flood of letters telling of her love, and urging him to keep working on the play. The content and tone of *The Three Sisters* reflect this epistolary dialogue, and in fact, participate in it, as critics like Emma Polotskaya and Zinovy Paperny have proven through close analysis of the text. Most notably, the sisters' refrain, "To Moscow! To Moscow!" reflects Chekhov's own state of mind as he worked on the play far from Olga, his friends, and the theater company in the city. The version he brought to them in October was incomplete, but the company began rehearsals, awaiting final revisions that he would complete in Nice, where he traveled in December. The play, which premiered at the end of January 1901, was another stunning success.

After spending the rest of the winter in Yalta in worsening health, Chekhov traveled to Moscow in spring, where, on May 25, 1901, he married Olga quietly in a church with just witnesses present. Never appreciative of formalities and public celebrations, he had asked a friend to arrange a reception for friends and family in a completely different location—with everyone present except the newly married couple. For a honeymoon, the two of them traveled to the Ural area, where Chekhov spent a few weeks taking the *kumys* (fermented mare's milk) treatment. Then, after a summer together in Yalta, Olga again left for Moscow, where the new theater season was to begin. Though Anton was able to visit her there for a short while in September, with the onset of cold weather at the end of October he had to flee southward.

These years marked Chekhov's greatest fame. Following a time-honored Russian literary tradition, his works, from "Fat and Thin"

(1883) to "Anna on the Neck" (1904) and "The Lady with the Dog," often satirize official ranks, commendations, and medals. But he received his own share of awards. In addition to prizes for his literary work (the Pushkin Prize for In the Twilight, 1888, and the Griboedov award for The Three Sisters, 1900-01), Chekhov was awarded the Order of St. Stanislav in 1899 for his contributions in the area of education. And in 1900, he was elected an honorary member of the Russian Academy of Sciences—not for science, but for literature. Within two years, though, after Gorky's election was annulled by the government (in connection with the writer's political radicalism), Chekhov, along with Vladimir Korolenko, resigned his membership in protest.

Critics have suggested that Chekhov's authorial presence grows in his later works. This is certainly true of his last two stories, "The Bishop" (1902) and "The Bride" (1903). The first tells the story of the last days in the life of a respected bishop. Doctors had sent him abroad to treat his health, to a town on the sea with a white church that recalls Nice. After eight years away, he returns home to Russia, having risen to a position of eminence. His new authority has created a distance between him and ordinary people, including his own mother, a simple peasant woman who is awkward in his presence and treats him formally. Only when she sees him ill and on the verge of death—which will take place, true to the Paschal (Easter) story frame, on Good Friday—does she share genuine emotion, love, and sorrow. In this way, Chekhov constructed the story of a man's life from birth to death—with his mother's presence at each end, at the gateway into and out of this world. As in many earlier stories, the reader sees through the eyes of the dying man ("A Boring Story," "Gusev," "Ward No. 6"). The exact moment of death is blurred, the point of view flips, the man's soul is released into the world, and readers are left outside with the bereaved mother, contemplating the discarded shell of the man's life. From her humble place in a remote village, she occasionally tells the other women about her children and grandchildren, and she would mention that she had had a son who'd been a bishop, "and she spoke timidly, fearing that they wouldn't believe her. ... And indeed not all of them did." The story reflects Chekhov's life path from low origins to a position of eminence; his relationship with his mother, who remained a woman of simple tastes and habits, who didn't read or appreciate his works, and who, as he surely knew, would survive him; his illness and travels to Nice; and the sounds, sights, and language of the church that, though he remained a committed scientist and empiricist throughout his life, inspired and permeated his writing.

Chekhov's last story, "The Bride," over and above its ostensible message in favor of women's independence, can be read as a love letter, gift, and farewell note to his wife. Even as such, the story bears his characteristic ironic touch. A young woman Nadya ("hope"), breaks off an engagement with a man who bores her, and flees her provincial town for St. Petersburg to get an education. The autobiographical hints are clear. In this bolt for freedom, she is urged on by Sasha, a family friend who had studied in Moscow, but spends summers with her family to relieve his tuberculosis. When after her first year of school she stops on her way home to visit him in his squalid room in Moscow, he is terribly thin, sicker than when she had seen him last, and his cough has gotten worse. Brimming with health, she looks ahead into the future; meanwhile, after leaving to take the *kumys* cure, he dies. She bids him farewell, "and before her eyes arose a new life, broad and spacious, and this life, as yet unclear, full of mystery, attracted her, beckoned." Full of life, she packs and leaves her home town forever—"or so she thought." The story's circular construction, with life continuing its patterns year to year, subject to the cycles of nature, renders any escape—from story, from provincial town, from routine, from life itself—a most uncertain matter. Hope, though, and the spirit of literature, persevere, and this Chekhov wills to Olga and to his readers.

Chekhov worked on his last play, *The Cherry Orchard*, through 1903—winter in Yalta, then spring in Moscow, then early summer in the countryside outside Moscow, and then back in Yalta in the summer and fall. The writing process was arduous, as his physical condition worsened day by day; he could only manage a few lines per day. Knowing the painful details of Chekhov's illness and his separation from Olga and MAT during much of this period, it is hard to view *The Cherry Orchard* as something light and funny, despite the playwright's insistence that it was a comedy, and despite its slapstick elements. The play's plot closely reflects the story of the Kiselyov family, Alexei and Maria, at whose estate of Babkino the Chekhovs had stayed in the summers in the mid-1880s. Representing the entire gentry landowning class, the Kiselyovs too ultimately lost their estate, and like Leonid Gaev in the play, Kiselyov took a job as director of a bank. Chekhov completed *The Cherry Orchard* and sent it to MAT in Moscow in October. He came to Moscow at the end of November and was able to attend rehearsals. The year 1904 marked the 25th anniversary of his literary activity—measured from his earliest publications. The play's premiere, on January 17, 1904, coincided with his 44th name day. (That is, the day in the Russian church calendar appointed for a saint. In Chekhov's case, the name day for St. Anton fell on his birthday). Under normal circumstances, the mood would be celebratory, but when he was called out to the stage during the third intermission to be honored with speeches and congratulations, emaciated and barely able to stand, the dire state of his health was obvious to everyone present. Like the premieres of his other plays, *The Cherry Orchard*'s opening night would be remembered as much for the atmosphere in the theater as for the performance onstage.

Within 14 years of *The Cherry Orchard*'s premiere—in the aftermath of the Bolshevik Revolution—the landed estates and their precarious, sensitive owners would no longer exist. Pyotr Trofimov, the young revolutionary who dreams only of the future ("all of Russia is our orchard") will leave this garden behind. Subsequent Russian and Soviet history would cast a dark shadow on his dream's bright tonality. Fortunately, the garden Chekhov depicted lives on, already in its second century, no less real now than when he wrote it all down, despite what historians might tell us. Literature is not a museum, but an experience that is renewed with each new reader.

The Cherry Orchard is, where it matters, the world in which we live today.

The writer's days were numbered, like those of his country. He spent the rest of the winter in Yalta, and joined Olga in Moscow in May. Despite the hopelessness of his condition and the stresses of travel, the two left for Germany at the beginning of June, where they alit in the spa town of Badenweiler. There, his illness progressed rapidly. On July 15 (on the Western calendar, July 2 in the Russian calendar), Olga called in a German doctor, who took Anton's pulse and immediately ordered a bottle of champagne. In doing so, he followed established custom: a doctor at a colleague's deathbed would offer champagne. Chekhov's last words were "*Ich sterbe*" [I'm dying] and, after taking a drink, "It's been a long time since I've had champagne."

And he left his shell behind.

8. Chekhov's Legacy

After Chekhov's death, his sister Masha lived in the white house in Yalta, where she preserved his archive for over half a century, caring for it through all the political changes of the 20th century, until her death in 1957. The Yalta Chekhov Museum survived two countries, imperial Russia and the Soviet Union, and remains open today, in uneasy Crimea. Olga continued to act, headlining productions of the Moscow Arts Theater, which thrived through the 20th century under its "seagull" logo. She died in 1959. MAT, with its Chekhov statue out front, continues to produce his plays, along with countless others.

Chekhov's characteristic restraint when it came to addressing political issues undoubtedly helped preserve his status as a revered Russian classic after the Bolshevik revolution, even as other writers fell out of favor. His stories and plays were part of the curriculum in Soviet schools, and continue to be taught today, 30 years after the collapse of the Soviet Union. He once told a friend that he would be forgotten within seven years after his death. The opposite has come to pass: Chekhov's fame continues to grow. Of all the world's writers, his works are among those most translated into foreign languages. His plays are at the center of acting training programs; no budding writer can make it through the Master of Fine Arts curriculum without studying his stories. Every year brings new productions on stage in the major theaters of the world, as well as in schools and universities, online, and in film. Performances run from reverential, classic portrayals that reproduce all the details of the first performances—including at MAT—to radical and avant-garde productions, both in rarified venues and out on the streets. In the winter of 2020, for example, unsuspecting travelers on an ordinary train from Chekhov's hometown of Taganrog to Moscow were treated to a celebration of the 160th anniversary of the writer's birth, with a marathon series of performances on board for the duration of the journey.

In Russia, the epithet most often applied to Chekhov is "human" or "humane." Sophisticated, cynical, or even merely thoughtful people may ask: all well and good, but what does that word actually mean? The 21st century has brought unprecedented challenges to humanity—a perfect storm of intertwined economic, cultural, political, environmental, and public health crises. At this moment, Chekhov's practice as a doctor, his "big data" exercise on Sakhalin, and his many contributions to public service, have come into renewed focus. With perspective, it is impossible to separate the literature from the man himself, the doctor, the citizen, the family man, the lover, and friend. He lived a life not that different from ours, despite the distance in time and space separating us, affirming by practice and example our common humanity.

The growing field of the Medical Humanities takes a holistic approach to healing, through a combination of scientific authority, global awareness, artistic appreciation, and boots-on-the-ground practice. Even the most cautious scientists have recognized the healing powers of story-telling, powers impossible to measure, and yet tangibly felt in the practice. This felt truth, elusive in the telling, was Chekhov's lifelong focus as a writer. Through his powers of observation, his uncompromising scientific mind, his extraordinary craftsmanship, and his ear for the music of language, he brought his characters, narrators, and readers to the edge of what the human mind can grasp, and then left them there with a story—the whole thing, not just the words—echoing in their ears. Reading his works and watching his plays is, above all, healing to the body, mind, and soul.

Sources

A ll quotes from Chekhov in this book are taken from the Russian Academy edition of his complete collected works, A. P. Chekhov, *Polnoe sobranie sochinenii i pisem*, 30 vols. (Moscow: "Nauka," 1974-1983), available online at http://feb-web.ru/feb/chekhov/default.asp. All translations are mine except the quotes from Chekhov's notebooks in Chapter 3, which are by Constance Garnett.

Chekhov's best-known stories and plays exist in multiple translations, scattered around in different collections. There is no consensus as to which English versions are best. Between 1916 and 1922, the famous British translator Constance Garnett produced 13 volumes of short stories and drama; these have appeared in various configurations in many editions, notably Ecco's lovingly produced *Tales of Chekhov* (2006). In the 1960s, Ronald Hingley translated the nine volumes of *The Oxford Chekhov*. Garnett's versions remain among the finest, featuring a fluent English style; Hingley's are quite free, with ambitious word choices that are sometimes controversial but never boring. *Anton Chekhov's Selected Stories*, edited by Cathy Popkin (Norton, 2014), is a superb collection, with works by a wide variety of translators, some of them commissioned especially for the volume. The Anton Chekhov Foundation is currently sponsoring the Early Chekhov Translation Project, a unique collaborative effort to produce the first comprehensive collection of Chekhov's earliest stories in English (http://antonchekhovfoundation.org/ectp.html).

The best way to get a sense of Chekhov's style is to read two or three versions of a particular work, side by side. Harvey Pitcher's and Patrick Miles's versions of early stories are among the best. Also, consult and compare translations by Ann Dunnigan and Avrahm Yarmolinsky, as well as Richard Pevear and Larissa Volokhonsky; these range from very free, with a concern for fluent English style, to literal and faithful to the original language structure and syntax.

Pevear/Volokhonsky's versions are known for the latter qualities. Recently, a number of Chekhov's longer stories have been appearing in single-volume editions, for example, by Hesperus Classics. Second-hand bookstores often have quirky old Chekhov collections well worth acquiring. Shun texts (including online versions) if the translator is not credited. These can be unreliable.

Translations of Chekhov's four major plays are often adapted and adjusted to the needs of a particular performance. To get an excellent sense for Chekhov's drama, compare translations by, in addition to Garnett and Hingley, Sharon Carnicke (Hackett, 2009); Peter Carson (Penguin Random House, 2002); Michael Heim (Modern Library, 2003); Michael Frayn (Bloomsbury, 1993); Paul Schmidt (HarperCollins, 1997); and Lawrence Senelick (Norton, 2004).

THE RUSSIAN LANGUAGE

As you explore Chekhov's works, you may notice that the same person or place may be spelled differently depending on the version you are reading. This is because Russian is written in the Cyrillic alphabet, and there is not a perfect match between their and our letters. Particular offenders here are the letters "i", "y", and "j"; many Russian family names, for example, end in "sky" (or "ski") and "skaya" (or "skaia"). The former marks a male, the latter a female. In this book I aimed for the spellings most comfortable and familiar for the English-language reader.

In the play *Uncle Vanya* (or *Uncle Vania*), the professor might be Serebryakov or Serebriakov; his daughter might be Sonya or Sonia. The professor's wife might be Yelena, Ellen, or Elena; the translator might even choose "Helen," to hint at a resonance, on grounds of beauty, with Helen of Troy. Words (including names) referring to females tend to end in "a" or "ia/ya" (pronounced "ah" or "yah").

Readers sometimes think that Russian names are confusing. They are not. Russian names consist of three parts: the first name, patronymic, and last (family) name. The patronymic is derived by adding -ovich/evich (for males) or -ovna/evna (for females) to the father's name. In formal speech, people call each other by the first name and patronymic. Thus, by paying attention to names, you will be able to use the patronymic to identify siblings (by a shared patronymic) and paternal relationships. In informal speech, nicknames (diminutives) are used.

Take, for example, the Prozorov family in *The Three Sisters*. Olga, Masha (diminutive for Maria), and Irina's patronymic is Sergeevna, which means their father's name was Sergei; their brother is Andrei Sergeevich. Andrei's wife Natasha (nickname for Natalya), who is prone to using diminutives, calls him Andryusha; speaking to her toddler son Bobik in Act IV, she refers to Olga as "Aunt Olya." Take note of the ways characters refer to one another and develop a sense of the levels of intimacy reflected in these terms of address.

Suggested Reading

LETTERS

There are several editions of Chekhov's letters in English translation. The two indispensable collections are:

> Anton Chekhov's Life and Thought: Selected Letters and Commentary, trans. Michael Henry Heim, in collaboration with Simon Karlinsky; selection, introduction and commentary by Simon Karlinsky (Northwestern University Press, 1997); originally published as Letters of Anton Chekhov (Harper & Row, 1973); and

> Anton Chekhov: A Life in Letters, ed. Rosamund Bartlett; trans. Rosamund Bartlett and Anthony Phillips (Penguin Classics, 2004).

> Jean Benedetti's short collection, Dear Writer, Dear Actress (Methuen, 2007), brings together letters that Chekhov exchanged with his wife, the actress Olga Knipper, during the last years of his life.

BIOGRAPHY

Chekhov's life is extremely well documented. Russian scholarship has produced superb materials such as the extraordinary Chronicle of Chekhov's Life and Works (http://chehov-lit.ru/chehov/bio/letopis/letopis.htm), a source originally published by N.I. Gitovich in 1955, and subsequently expanded to include most of the documents available that relate to Chekhov's day-to-day life from birth to death. Everything is online: here you can also find links to the writer's letters, literary works, notebooks, and even one-line inscriptions he wrote in books he gave to people. The curious are urged to click on links in this source; copy and paste the Russian text that pops up into google-translate to see what's there. Chekhov's father kept a diary, meticulously noting down daily events during the family's years in Melikhovo. This diary is available online at http://az.lib.ru/c/chehow_a_p/text_0470.shtml. Memoirs and letters are key sources; Chekhov himself meticulously saved the letters he received, filing them in folders every year. Unfortunately, his letters to others were not always treated with the same respect; thus in some important cases, we are left with only one side of the epistolary dialogue. Missing, tragically, are most of the letters teenage Anton wrote to his family when they left him alone in Taganrog between the ages of 16 and 19), as well as the letters he wrote to the painter Isaac Levitan, with whom he was very close both as a human being and an artist. On the positive side, once he became famous, correspondents showed him more care. The letters he exchanged with his wife Olga offer an important window into his last years, and read like an epistolary romance. Unlike many writers, Chekhov did not keep a diary, and though his notebooks are extremely valuable for the insights they provide into his creative process, they constitute only a very small part of his body of writing (one short volume in the collected works). Chekhov's letters are particularly important. At 12 volumes, they are his largest body of writings, compared with 10 volumes of prose, three of drama, and five volumes of miscellaneous works (including the non-fictional *Sakhalin Island*). The letters are valuable as a source of information about his life, his professional and personal relationships, his views about the world around him, and about his own artistic stance. They serve as a workshop for his writing craft, and their language often spills over into his fiction and drama. Most importantly, Chekhov's letters can be read as an integral work of art in their own right, a great "novel of life" by the one Russian classic prose writer who never wrote a novel.

Donald Rayfield, *Anton Chekhov: A Life* (HarperCollins, 1997) is the most comprehensive and authoritative biography in English.

Rosamund Bartlett, *Chekhov: Scenes from a Life* (The Free Press, 2004), considers Chekhov's life in the context of the places where he lived and traveled.

Patrick Miles, *Brief Lives: Anton Chekhov* (Hesperus, 2008). A marvelous short biography that covers the highlights.

Readable and engaging earlier biographies include:

Ronald Hingley, *Chekhov: A Biographical and Critical Study* (Allen & Unwin, 1950)

Ronald Hingley, *A Life of Chekhov* (Oxford, 1989)

Ernest Simmons, *Chekhov. A Biography* (Little, Brown, 1962).

MEMOIRS

Much of what we know about Chekhov comes from memoirs of people close to him. They bring with them a unique personal perspective that reflects not only the authors' recollections of Chekhov, but also their distinct point of view and even agenda. Read these to get a sense of Chekhov's relationships with important people, as well as to learn facts about his life.

Mikhail Chekhov, *Anton Chekhov: A Brother's Memoir*, tr. Eugene Alper (St. Martin's, 2009)

Anton Chekhov and his Times, comp. and with an introduction by Andrei Turkov; tr. Cynthia Carlile and Sharon McKee (University of Arkansas Press, 1995) offers an excellent sampling of letters and reminiscences.

Ivan Bunin, *About Chekhov: The Unfinished Symphony*, tr. Thomas Gaiton Marullo (Northwestern, 2007)

Maxim Gorky, Alexander Kuprin, Ivan Bunin, *Reminiscences of Anton Chekhov* (Wildside, 2011)

Memories of Chekhov, ed. Peter Sekirin (McFarland, 2011), is a "documentary biography" comprising over a hundred written recollections of the writer.

SCHOLARSHIP, REFERENCE WORKS, and CRITICISM

Some of the best articles about Chekhov's writing are scattered in a wide variety of academic journals. The following list gives a good sampling of book-length studies; take a look and then explore the bibliographies to discover other work by critics and scholars you like. Criticism necessarily represents a single point of view, so nothing you find here is the "last word," just part of a long and exciting conversation that you are welcome to join.

Anton Chekhov Rediscovered: A Collection of New Studies with a Comprehensive Bibliography, ed. Savely Senderovich and Munir Sendich (Russian Language Journal, 1987)

Approaches to Teaching the Works of Anton Chekhov, ed. Michael C. Finke and Michael Holquist (MLA, 2016) – a valuable and accessible collection of short essays by experts aimed at a general audience of readers and teachers

The Cambridge Companion to Chekhov, ed. Vera Gottlieb (Cambridge, 2006) – a collection of essays that focuses on Chekhov's dramatic works

Chekhov and Our Age: Responses to Chekhov by American

Writers and Scholars, ed. James McConkey (Center for International Studies, Cornell, 1985)

A Chekhov Companion, ed. Toby W. Clyman (Greenwood, 1985)

Chekhov for the Twenty-First Century, ed. Carol Apollonio and Angela Brintlinger (Slavica, 2012)

Chekhov the Immigrant: Translating a Cultural Icon, ed. Michael C. Finke and Julie de Sherbinin (Slavica, 2008)

Chekhov: Poetics, Hermeneutics, Thematics, ed. J. Douglas Clayton (Slavic Research Group, University of Ottawa, 2006)

Chekhov's Letters: Biography, Context, Poetics, ed. Carol Apollonio and Radislav Lapushin (Lexington [Crosscurrents], 1918)

Critical Essays on Anton Chekhov, ed. Thomas Eekman, Thomas (G. K. Hall, 1989)

Kenneth Lantz, *Anton Chekhov: A Reference Guide* (G K Hall, 1985)

Lauren Leighton, *A Bibliography of Anton Chekhov in English* (Edwin Mellen, 2005)

Reading Chekhov's Text, ed. Robert Louis Jackson (Northwestern, 1993)

SINGLE-AUTHOR BOOKS

Peter M. Bitsilli, *Chekhov's Art: A Stylistic Analysis*, trans. Toby W. Clyman and Edwina Jannie Cruise (Ardis, 1983) – a classic Russian study of Chekhov's style

Alexander Chudakov, *Chekhov's Poetics*, trans. Edwina Jannie Cruise (Ardis, 1983) – a beautiful analysis of Chekhov's narrative technique

Julie de Sherbinin, *Chekhov and Russian Religious Culture: The Poetics of the Marian Paradigm* (Northwestern, 1997) – an exploration of Chekhov's use of biblical images of Mary

Michael Finke, *Metapoesis in Pushkin, Gogol, Dostoevskii and Chekhov* (Indiana, 1989)

Michael Finke, *Seeing Chekhov: Life and Art* (Cornell, 2005) – a subtle analysis of the relationship between the writer's creative work and his strategies for preserving his privacy as a human being

Richard Gilman, *Chekhov's Plays: An Opening into Eternity* (Yale, 1996) – readings of Chekhov's major plays

Serge Gregory, *Antosha and Levitasha: The Shared Lives and Art of Anton Chekhov* (Northern Illinois, 2015) – a study of the close personal and artistic relationship between Chekhov and the premier Russian landscape artist of his time

Vladimir Kataev, *If Only we Could Know! An Interpretation of Chekhov*, trans. Harvey Pitcher, (Ivan R. Dee, 2003) – a classic work of Russian criticism addressing Chekhov's epistemology

Daria A. Kirjanov, *Chekhov and the Poetics of Memory* (Peter Lang, 2000) – subtle textual readings of Chekhov's stories

Karl D. Kramer, *The Chameleon and the Dream: The Image of Reality in Chekhov's Stories* (The Hague: Mouton, 1970) – a classic collection

Radislav Lapushin, *"Dew on the Grass" The Poetics of*

Inbetweenness in Chekhov (Peter Lang, 2010) – an analysis of the poetic language of Chekhov's works

Janet Malcolm, *Reading Chekhov: A Critical Journey* (Random House, 2002) – literary travelogue to Chekhov landmarks

Richard Peace, *Chekhov: A Study of the Four Major Plays* (Yale, 1983)

Cathy Popkin, *The Pragmatics of Insignificance: Chekhov, Zoshchenko, Gogol* (Stanford, 1994)

Donald Rayfield, *Understanding Chekhov: A Critical Study of Chekhov's Prose and Drama* (University of Wisconsin, 1999)

Lawrence Senelick, *The Chekhov Theater: A Century of the Plays in Performance* (Cambridge, 1997)

Mark Stanley Swift, *Biblical Subtexts and Religious Themes in the Works of Anton Chekhov* (Peter Lang, 2003) – an analysis of primarily Old Testament subtexts

Maurice Valencey, *The Breaking String: The Plays of Anton Chekhov* (Oxford: Oxford UP, 1966)

Thomas Winner, *Chekhov and his Prose* (Holt, Reinhard and Winston 1966)

About the Author

Carol Apollonio is the author, editor, and co-editor of numerous books about Russian literature, including *Chekhov's Letters* (2018), *Chekhov for the 21st Century* (2012), *The New Russian Dostoevsky* (2010), and *Dostoevsky's Secrets* (2009). Currently President of the International Dostoevsky Society, Apollonio holds a Chekhov Centennial medal from the Russian Ministry of Culture. In the fall of 2019, she followed Dostoevsky's and Chekhov's trail across Russia to Sakhalin Island, chronicling her adventures in the blog "Chekhov's Footprints." Apollonio teaches at Duke University.

A Word from the Publisher

Thank you for reading *Simply Chekhov*.

If you enjoyed reading it, we would be grateful if you could help others discover and enjoy it too.

Please review it with your favorite book provider such as Amazon, BN, Kobo, Apple Books, or Goodreads, among others.

Again, thank you for your support and we look forward to offering you more great reads.

9 781943 657544